MODERN
NATIONS
—OF THE—
WORLD

IRAQ

IRAQ

MODERN NATIONS —OF THE— WORLD

IRAQ

BY PHYLLIS CORZINE

LUCENT BOOKS®

THOMSON
─ ✳ ─
™
GALE

San Diego • Detroit • New York • San Francisco • Cleveland
New Haven, Conn. • Waterville, Maine • London • Munich

© 2003 by Lucent Books. Lucent Books is an imprint of The Gale Group, Inc.,
a division of Thomson Learning, Inc.

Lucent Books® and Thomson Learning™ are trademarks used herein under license.

For more information, contact
Lucent Books
27500 Drake Rd.
Farmington Hills, MI 48331-3535
Or you can visit our Internet site at http://www.gale.com

LIBRARY OF CONGRESS CATALOGING-IN-PUBLICATION DATA

Corzine, Phyllis, 1943–
   Iraq / by Phyllis Corzine.
     v. cm. — (Modern nations of the world)
  Includes bibliographical references and index.
  Summary: Discusses the Iraqi people and culture; Iraq as the "cradle of civilization";
Western influence; problems facing modern Iraq.
   ISBN 1-59018-114-X
   1. Iraq—Juvenile literature. [1. Iraq.] I. Title. II. Series.
   DS70.62 .C67 2003
   956.7—dc21

                                  2002014471

CONTENTS

INTRODUCTION

ANCIENT LAND—MODERN NATION

The geography of Iraq—its mountains and marshes, rivers, deserts, and plains—has shaped its history and its people. Much of the land that is now Iraq lies between the Tigris and Euphrates rivers. It is part of what the ancient Greeks called *Mesopotamia*—"land between the rivers." The waters of these two rivers made it possible for wandering groups of prehistoric people to settle down and grow crops, build villages and towns, and finally develop one of the world's first civilizations.

For thousands of years, the ancient land that encompasses the modern nation of Iraq has been the site both of brilliant civilizations and of devastating destruction. The land of Mesopotamia is of two types—the flat, arid land in the south, and the rolling, greener region in the north. In the southern region—the land between the rivers—ancient Sumerians established the first city life nearly 6,000 years ago. Over the next 4,000 years Sumer developed into a vibrant and complex civilization. Writing, literature, laws, mathematics, agriculture, and government planning and administration first appeared here. At times throughout its thousands of years of history, Mesopotamia was the center of the civilized world. However, at other times, the region was a near-wasteland, destroyed by invading armies that moved on and left its people to recover and survive as best they could. At still other times, it was an unimportant and neglected part of a much larger empire.

Although Mesopotamia was the home of civilization for thousands of years, the modern nation of Iraq did not emerge in the region until 1920. In that year, British statesman Sir Winston Churchill and other British officials met to draw the lines of the nation of Iraq. The Ottoman Empire had ruled the region for nearly 500 years, until 1918 when Britain and its allies defeated the Ottomans in World War I. Britain gained control of the region, and Iraq did not achieve independence from British rule until 1932.

The land that the British shaped into the modern state of Iraq was made up of three provinces under the Ottomans. Basra in the south was home mainly to Arabs belonging to the Shia branch of the Islamic religion. Basra province also contained the vast marshlands that were home to the Marsh Arabs, descendants of ancient peoples, who also belonged to the Shia branch of Islam. In the center was the province of Baghdad, home to many Arabs belonging to the Sunni branch of Islam. In the north was the mountainous province of Mosul, home of the Kurdish people, who speak their own language and have a distinct culture. Through the centuries, these ethnic and religious groups were enemies and have often been at war. Under British rule, they became one nation. But these centuries-old divisions remain and continue to cause conflict in the twenty-first century.

Much of modern Iraq's history has been as tumultuous as its past. Even though the Iraqi nation is less than 100 years old, it has been the scene of bloody uprisings and popular movements for independence and freedom from

An ancient Sumerian tablet describes the sale of a field and house paid for in silver. The Sumerians lived in southern Mesopotamia, now known as Iraq.

British influence. Finally, in 1968, the Iraqi Baath Party took control of the government. Saddam Hussein, the head of the Baath Party and Iraq's president, came to power in 1979.

Saddam Hussein did not bring peace and prosperity to his country, however. With the wealth from its vast oil reserves, Iraq built one of the most powerful armies in the Arab world. Then in 1980, Saddam launched a war against neighboring Iran. In 1990 Saddam invaded the neighboring nation of Kuwait, triggering the Persian Gulf War between Iraq and the United States and its allies. And Iraq may soon be involved in yet another and even more devastating war, once again with the United States and its allies.

Saddam Hussein makes his first public appearance as president in 1979. Under Saddam, Iraq has not experienced peace or prosperity.

Now, once again, Iraq is the center of world attention, but not as a center of civilization. Today, Iraq is considered by many other nations of the world as an outlaw nation. Saddam Hussein is thought of as a threat to world peace. Other world leaders believe he may be trying to develop terrible biological, chemical, and even nuclear weapons that could destroy masses of people.

Even though Iraq today is suffering under Saddam Hussein's leadership, the nation has the potential to once again be a prosperous center of civilization. Iraq is rich in oil, with 10 percent of the world's oil reserves. The broad plains between the Tigris and Euphrates rivers are fertile lands capable of producing abundant crops. Iraq has the potential for a thriving manufacturing industry, which is now crippled by lack of materials.

Despite the world community's disapproval of Saddam Hussein, it is well to remember that the land that he rules is, indeed, the cradle of civilization and that the Western world owes much to ancient Mesopotamia. As author Geoff Simons explains,

> We often tend to begin the chronicle of Western culture
> with the achievements of the classical world, but it is
> worth remembering that the Greco-Roman states owe
> much to the ancient worlds of Egypt and Mesopotamia,
> [which are] as far removed in time from [Greece and
> Rome] as Greece and Rome are [removed] from the na-
> tion states of the modern era. We may reflect also that a
> modern Iraqi is entitled to contemplate with awe and
> pride the [fruitful] richness of the cultures that first
> emerged in his land more than five thousand years ago.[1]

1

IRAQ—THE LAND AND ITS CITIES

The modern nation of Iraq is located in southwestern Asia at the head of the Persian Gulf. It covers nearly 168,000 square miles—slightly larger than the state of California. The nations of Syria and Jordan border Iraq on the west, and Saudi Arabia and Kuwait form the southern border. To the north, Iraq is bordered by Turkey and to the east by Iran.

GEOGRAPHY

Iraq has four major geographical regions: northern plain, southern plain, mountains, and desert. Between the Tigris and Euphrates rivers just north of the city of Samarra lies the dry northern plain. This region is sometimes called Al-Jazirah ("The Island"). The highest of these rolling hills reaches 1,000 feet above sea level. Small streams cut deep, narrow routes through jagged hills. The deep valleys make the land difficult to irrigate, but there are a few farming villages in the region. Farther to the north and northeast, Iraq is flanked by the Zagros and Taurus mountain ranges. The Zagros Mountains extend into Iran, and the Taurus Mountains divide Iraq from Turkey. Many peaks reach above 9,000 feet, and some reach as high as 11,000 feet. The Kurds, Iraq's largest non-Arab population group, live in the valleys and foothills, in the region called Kurdistan. These high mountain regions contain the only forests in Iraq.

The southern plain stretches from Samarra southeast to the Persian Gulf. The plain is alluvial, which means that it is built up of clay, sand, rocks, and sediment laid down by centuries of river floods. The area includes the fertile delta between the mouths of the Tigris and Euphrates rivers. Most of Iraq's people live in this region. This was the land that people first settled. Although the land receives little rain, it is fertile and has plenty of water from the rivers for irrigating crops.

In the far south, the plain becomes a marshy swampland covered with palm trees and marsh reeds. In some areas, rushes, or reeds, can grow twenty feet high. The marshes cover about 6,000 square miles, extending east of the Tigris River and across the Iranian border. The marshes are flooded during the rainy season, and the land is dotted with islands constructed by the Madan, or Marsh Arabs, where they make their home. Much of the land becomes dry during the summer season. For most of the year, travel through the marshes is possible only by boat.

In the west and southwest lie vast deserts of limestone hills and sand dunes. In fact, nearly 40 percent of the country is desert. Most of the desert region is part of the Syrian Desert. In the southwest is the Al-Hajara Desert, which extends into Saudi Arabia. Throughout the desert are watercourses or narrow valleys called *wadi*. These are dry riverbeds throughout most of the year, but during winter rains they fill up and become swiftly moving rivers.

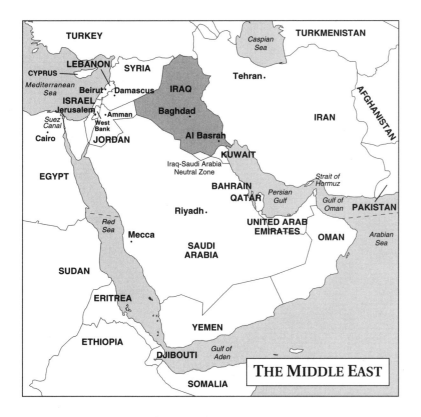

RIVERS

Iraq's two great rivers—the Tigris and the Euphrates—have been an important resource to the land for thousands of years. Carrying rich soil to the alluvial plains and providing water for irrigating crops, they gave birth to the world's earliest civilization. Both rivers rise out of the highlands of Turkey, where they are fed by melting snows. At one point, the two rivers come within about 20 miles of each other. They then spread apart until the valley between them is about 250 miles wide.

Both rivers are subject to serious flooding. Because of the many tributaries that carry water down from the mountains and feed the Tigris, it is subject to flash floods and can rise as much as 12 inches in an hour. Along its course, many old channels can be seen that were carved out by the flooding river. Unlike some other great rivers such as the Nile, the flooding of the rivers is unpredictable and can happen anytime between early April and early June. Not only the time but the extent of the flood cannot be predicted. Today, dams and irrigation systems help control the flooding of the southern plains and provide water for agriculture.

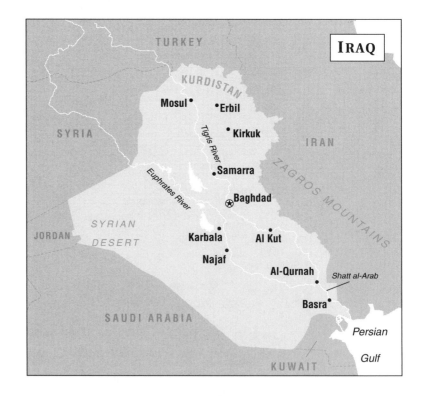

The Tigris and Euphrates rivers converge in southern Iraq at the town of al-Qurnah to form the Shatt al-Arab River. This waterway flows 115 miles southeast to the Persian Gulf, forming part of the border with Iran. For centuries, the Shatt al-Arab has been an important waterway for navigation and shipping.

CLIMATE

Iraq has two main climate regions: the hot, dry lowlands, which include the plains and deserts, and the cooler, damper northeast, which includes the rolling hills, or highlands, and the mountain ranges.

The lowland plains and deserts have hot, dry, cloudless summers. Temperatures in the deserts average over 90° F during the summer months. Summer lasts from May through October. During the hottest months of July and August, temperatures in the capital of Baghdad regularly reach 100° F, and temperatures as high as 123° F have been recorded. Winter begins in December and lasts through February. Winter temperatures are mild, with occasional frost. In Baghdad, winter temperatures range from 35° F to 60° F.

Summers in the high mountains are cool, with sharp temperature drops at night. In the hills of the northeast, summers are shorter than in the lowlands, lasting from June to September. Northeast summers are also slightly cooler. They are still hot and dry but average 5° to 10° F cooler than in the lowlands. The mountainous regions of Iraq have cold winters with occasional heavy snow. Winters in the highlands are very cold as well, with temperatures in some areas ranging between 24° and 63° F and sometimes falling into the teens.

Rainfall in most of Iraq is sparse and occurs mainly in the winter. Between 4 and 7 inches of rain falls annually in the lowlands, most of it between November and April. No rain falls from June through September, making irrigation of croplands necessary. In the highlands, between 12 and 20 inches of rain falls annually, most of it in the winter. Rainfall in the highlands is enough to water pastureland. The mountains receive more moisture, much of it in the form of snow.

Iraq has two types of winds. A dry, hot wind from the south and southeast is called the *sharki*. It blows during the change of seasons—early summer and early winter. A second type of

DUST STORMS AND THE DJINN

In the deserts of Iraq, as in the Syrian desert in the west, dust storms are common occurrences. Dust storms are not to be confused with sandstorms, which are low clouds of moving sand generally no higher than 10 feet. A dust storm is a wall of moving dust that can tower over a mile high. These storms are usually short-lived but have been known to last as long as 12 hours.

In ancient times, the people of the Middle East attributed these violent storms to *djinn* (pronounced "jin"). The djinn were mythical creatures that resemble western fairies. (In English we know them as genies.) People believed that dust storms were the work of an angry or evil djinn stirring up trouble.

wind called the *shamal* blows from the north and northwest, bringing dry air and cloudless skies, which intensely heats up the land surface. Dust storms occur regularly in Iraq, especially with the sharki. The storms turn the sky a reddish color and cover everything with a film of fine sand. In severe storms, thick clouds of dust can rise several thousand feet in the air, forcing airports to close.

PLANTS

The extreme dryness and heat throughout much of Iraq limit the plant life that can survive. Much of the natural vegetation includes low-growing shrubs, which can live year round and can survive the extreme heat, and flowering plants that bloom into brilliant colors after the winter rains and then wilt under the summer sun. Date palms are found nearly everywhere in Iraq. Bulrushes, which are tall reeds, and grasslike plants grow along riverbanks and marshes in southern Iraq. The licorice plant grows along the rivers. Licorice flavoring used in candy and other sweets is extracted from the underground stems of the plant.

The northern mountains of Iraq were once covered with thick oak forests. However, the forests have gradually disappeared as the trees were cut for firewood and charcoal, and the land was used for grazing. Some areas that were once forested are now scrubland, although other areas support stands of maple and pine.

ANIMALS

The land between the rivers was once home to lions, a type of antelope called the oryx, and other large animals. However, centuries of human occupation have driven out much of the larger wildlife. A few wild donkeys and ostrich still roam the dry lands today. Other animals that inhabit Iraq are wolves, hyenas, wildcats, and foxes. Gazelle and wild pigs are found in remote areas. Small animals such as badgers and otters can be found in the wet areas. Fish are an important part of the Iraqi diet, and rivers, streams, and lakes support a variety of fish, including carp and catfish.

Drought-resistant date palms can be seen throughout Iraq's dry landscape.

A wide variety of birds inhabit Iraq or visit it seasonally, escaping the cold European winters. The mountainous north is home to a variety of birds of prey, such as hawks, falcons, vultures, and owls. In south and central Iraq, the singing nightingale and the colorful "bride of the orchard" can be found in the date palm plantations and orange and pomegranate orchards. In the marshes, waterfowl are abundant. Ducks, geese, and even the giant white pelican can be found fishing in the warm waters. The creatures most at home in Iraq's climate are the many snakes and lizards that live in the desert areas.

Iraq's domesticated animals include camels, oxen, horses, and water buffalo. In the north large flocks of sheep and goats graze in the highlands, supplying wool and skins.

BAGHDAD—CAPITAL CITY OF IRAQ

Iraq is a sprawling land, with vast empty deserts and sparsely populated mountainous regions. The majority of Iraq's people live in cities. The largest and most important city is Baghdad, the capital of Iraq. Covering a little more than 250 square miles and with a population near 5 million, Baghdad is also one of the largest cities in the Middle East. (By comparison, New York City has about 7.5 million people, and Los Angeles has about 3.5 million.) The city lies roughly in the middle of the country. It is a little over 350 miles northeast of the Persian Gulf and sits astride the Tigris River, which runs through it. The river is spanned by eleven bridges connecting the two sides of the city. Baghdad has been the capital of the area since the city was founded in the eighth century by the Abbasid ruler Al-Mansur. The majority of Baghdad's inhabitants are Muslim Arabs.

Baghdad is the economic and cultural center of Iraq. Extending out from the center of the city are factories and residential areas. Industries include food processing; cement, textile, and cigarette manufacturing; and petroleum refining. Baghdad is also the hub of busy air, highway, and railroad systems that connect the city to the Persian Gulf and to other nations.

The oldest part of the city lies on the east bank of the Tigris. Its narrow streets are lined with open-air shops. These rows of shops, or bazaars, sell handcrafted items such as cloth, jewelry, leather goods, and rugs. Despite Baghdad's fabled and romantic place in the collection of stories known as *The Thousand*

ATA ALLAH: THE AMAZING CAMEL

Desert nomads have used camels for thousands of years. *Ata Allah,* meaning "God's gift," is the Bedouin name for the one-hump camel. Since motor vehicles are now commonly used in desert travel, the camel is not as important as it once was. However, in many parts of the world, including Iraq, camels are still highly valued. A few nomadic Bedouin still rely upon the camel, as they have for generations.

The camel is the ideal method of transportation for the nomadic Bedouin, who travel long distances over the arid land. Camels can go up to a week without water or food. After having gone without water, a single camel can drink as much as 21 gallons of water in 10 minutes, an amount that would kill another animal. Contrary to popular belief, camels do not store water in their humps, but they do store fatty tissue in the hump that the animal draws on in leaner times. If a camel is forced to go without food for any length of time, the hump will shrink and hang limply until the animal can feed again. The camel can eat almost anything—thornbushes, bones, dried leaves—a definite advantage when traveling through desert lands.

In addition to surviving for long periods of time without water and food, camels have several other adaptations for desert life that make them useful to the nomadic Bedouin. Their eyes are protected from sand by a double row of eyelashes, their ears are lined with fur to keep sand out, and their nasal passages can be opened and closed as needed. Camels can even raise their body's temperature tolerance to conserve body fluids.

Bedouin have long used camels not just for transportation but as a source of survival. They use camel hair for their tents and rugs, camel milk (which is more nutritious than cow's milk), and the meat of the camel.

Nomadic Bedouin depend on the hardy camel for survival.

BAGHDAD, THE ROUND CITY

Today the city of Baghdad is a plain city, bomb damaged, with many streets of dreary concrete buildings. Although there are some impressive modern buildings and monuments, there are few hints of its glorious past. But in 762, when al-Mansur, the second caliph of the Abbasid dynasty, built his capital on the west bank of the Tigris River, this city of Baghdad became the glittering center of Islamic civilization during its golden age. Al-Mansur named this city Madinat al-Salaam ("City of Peace"), but it was known to many as "the Round City" because of its circular walls.

The city was built with three round walls, one inside the other. In the center was the caliph's palace with its famous Great Dome. When the caliph received visitors in his palace, a soldier always stood by his throne with a sharp sword, ready to behead any visitor who displeased the caliph.

From the center circle of the city, four avenues extended, dividing the city into four quarters. The four avenues radiating from the center of the city passed through four gates and led to various parts of the Islamic empire.

Between the palace wall and the middle wall was the business district. Baghdad was on the major caravan route from India and China. In markets along the four avenues, merchants sold glassware from Syria, silk from China, rubies from India, and leather goods from Spain. By the year 1000, Baghdad was considered one of the richest cities in the world, with a population of about 1,000,000.

and One Nights, most of its buildings date from the end of World War I or later, especially on the west bank of the Tigris. The income from oil following World War II led to a flurry of new building as well, and Baghdad can boast many modern buildings, such as banks, hotels, and department stores. Baghdad also contains many modern monuments, such as the monument in the shape of a modernistic shield, which commemorates the Unknown Soldier, and the Martyr's Monument, a dome that commemorates the dead of the Iraq-Iran war.

A few historically important structures remain in Baghdad. The Abbasid Palace (named for the Abbasid dynasty of Islamic rulers who occupied the palace) dates from about 1179. The palace was probably originally an Islamic college. It features carved, decorative brickwork and a large hall with a vaulted ceiling nearly 30 feet high. The most famous historical building in Baghdad is the Mustansiriyah Madrassa (or college), built between 1227 and 1233. The madrassa was founded by the Caliph al-Mustansir and contained four law schools. The building is rectangular with a central courtyard. It has four large halls, walled on three sides, with the fourth side open, facing the courtyard. The halls have vaulted ceilings and are covered with decorative brickwork. Both the Abbasid Palace and the Mustansiriyah Madrassa are now museums.

Another important historical building is the Mirjan Mosque. It was built in 1358, next to an important Islamic college, which has since been destroyed. The mosque is built around a huge central courtyard, which is covered with a series of giant vaults. Windows in the vaults let in natural light to illuminate the large central area.

One of the most striking features of modern Baghdad is the face of Iraqi president Saddam Hussein, which seems to be everywhere. His portrait appears on walls of buildings—inside and out—throughout the city. Stone, bronze, and cast-metal statues of Saddam are on nearly every block. In front of a government building stands a 20-foot-tall bronze statue of Saddam. Portraits show Saddam in military uniform staring through binoculars, wearing a business suit and smiling, wearing Iraqi national dress, and smoking a cigar.

Two women walk past a wall mural of Saddam Hussein. Countless buildings in Baghdad are covered with the Iraqi president's image.

BASRA

Basra is Iraq's second largest city and sits on the western bank of the Shatt al-Arab waterway, which empties directly into the Persian Gulf, just 55 miles to the southeast. Basra is Iraq's principal port for the export and import of goods. It was also a major petroleum refining and exporting center before the wars of the 1980s and 1990s damaged the facilities. Its population also declined during that period, from a high of 1.5 million in 1977 to less than 900,000 in the late 1980s. Although it was rebuilt, it was again heavily damaged during the Persian Gulf War in 1991, and later during the fighting between Iraqi government troops and rebel groups.

Basra was founded in A.D. 637 by Arabs as a military base. It was a center of culture throughout the eighth and ninth centuries, when it was the home of noted Arab poets and scholars. During the sixteenth century Basra was an important port for Arab trading ships traveling to the Far East.

The modern city of Basra has three main areas. Ashar is the old commercial district, which contains bazaars, along with old houses with balconies over the narrow streets. Margil is the port district, which also has some modern residential areas. Basra proper is the old residential area with many beautiful homes. Palm groves surround these settlements. The city of Basra figures in the stories of Sinbad the Sailor in *The Thousand and One Nights.*

OTHER CITIES OF IRAQ

Mosul is sometimes called the "pearl of the north" and is one of Iraq's largest cities, with approximately 665,000 inhabitants. It is located on the banks of the Tigris River, north of Baghdad. Mosul became an important trade center because of its position along a caravan route between the Mediterranean and Persia and India. The city's most important export was once fine cotton goods. Muslin, a fine cotton cloth, was named for the city. Since the 1930s, Mosul has been an important center because of the oil production in the region.

Mosul is an ethnically diverse city, with a majority of Kurds. The city is also home to large numbers of Assyrians and Turkomen, as well as Arabs. Although most of Mosul's inhabitants are Muslims, the city has the largest Christian population in Iraq, and it is the site of many old Christian churches and old mosques.

Erbil (also spelled Arbil or Irbil) is one of the oldest continuously settled sites in the world. It is located in northern Iraq, about 50 miles east of Mosul. Founded by the Sumerians about 2500 B.C., it later became an important center in ancient Assyria. The Assyrians called it Arba-Ilu, which means "City of the Four Gods." The modern city is on a high mound topped by a citadel, or *qala*, and rises 100 feet over the surrounding plain. The citadel was important during the Ot-

OIL BENEATH THE SANDS

Huge deposits of petroleum, also known as crude oil, have been found in what is now Iraq. Crude oil is produced by tiny organisms that lived and died in the world's oceans millions of years ago. Over time, their remains became trapped in the sediment (mud and sand) of the ocean bottom. As oceans dried up, these sediments were trapped beneath the earth's crust. High temperature and pressure caused them to compress, eventually creating oil and natural gas, which became trapped in reservoirs close to the earth's surface. Some regions of the earth are particularly rich in oil, and the Middle East is

among the richest. The entire region, including areas of Saudi Arabia, Kuwait, Iraq, and Iran, is rich in oil, but some fields are larger than others. Iraq has one of the four largest oil fields in the world near the city of Kirkuk. (Two of the other three are in Saudi Arabia and Iran.) Recently, new explorations have revealed even larger oil deposits than previously thought.

Oil fields like this one in Basra abound in Iraq and the Middle East.

toman period, and it contains many charming, old Turkish buildings. Today the city is the center of an agricultural area, where crops include sesame, corn, and fruit. The city is also the center of Iraqi Kurdistan, and most of its nearly half-million inhabitants are Kurds.

Another important city is Kirkuk, located about 145 miles north of Baghdad at the foot of the Zagros Mountains. Its population includes Turkomen, Kurds, Assyrians, and Arabs. The old city is built on a mound that is the site of a settlement dating to about 3000 B.C. Kirkuk is an important trade and export center for agriculture and has a small textile industry. Its main importance, however, is as a hub for the petroleum industry. Pipelines from Kirkuk carry oil westward to ports on the Mediterranean Sea.

Iraq is also home to several religious sites sacred to different sects of Islam. The city of Kerbala (or Karbala) is one such site, sacred to Shiite Muslims. In A.D. 680, the Sunni and Shia sects fought a battle at Kerbala. The leader of the Shiites, Hussein ibn Ali, and his brother Abbas were both killed. They were the prophet Muhammad's grandsons. Two shrines were built in their memory. Today the shrines are visited by devout Muslim pilgrims, many of whom are from Pakistan, Iran, India, and Afghanistan. Another city, Najaf, is the site of a mosque that contains the tomb of Ali, cousin and son-in-law of Muhammad and founder of the Shia sect of Islam. The site is regarded by Shiites as a holy place. Like Kerbala, Najaf is visited by thousands of Muslim pilgrims annually.

Throughout history, the geography of this ancient land has affected the lives of the people who lived here, as well as where and how they built their cities. Today, Iraq is still home to diverse groups of people who try to create a life for themselves in a harsh climate.

THE PEOPLE OF IRAQ

When the British drew the boundaries of the new nation of Iraq in 1920, they paid little attention to the natural boundaries of the homelands of ethnic groups in the region. Included today in Iraq's population of nearly 24 million people are several different ethnic groups. Even though most of the groups have lived in the region for many centuries, they maintain separate cultures and sometimes separate languages. These differences, as well as the hostility that exists between the Arabs, who are the majority, and some of the minority groups, are obstacles to maintaining a unified nation.

ARABS

Since the seventh century, when the region that is now Iraq came under the Arab Empire, Arabs have been the largest ethnic group in the region. Today, 75 to 80 percent of Iraq's population is Arab, and Arabic is the country's official language. The term *Arab* originally referred to the nomadic, camel-herding inhabitants of the Arabian Peninsula. In modern times, according to a Middle Eastern scholar, "Arabs are those who speak Arabic as their native tongue and who identify themselves as Arabs." [2] The number of nomadic people has shrunk over the years, and only 1 percent or less are nomads. Today, the term *Arab* has expanded to include about 200 million people who live in the Arab world, most of them in cities or towns. Most Arabs are Muslims—people who practice the religion of Islam.

Prior to the twentieth century, when the idea of nationalism (identification with a country) became popular, most Arabs identified themselves with their tribe, village, or town. Traditionally, Arabs in Iraq and elsewhere place a high value on family and family ties. Iraqi Arabs often live in extended families, with several generations living together, especially in rural areas. Houses in rural areas are usually made of mud brick or stone. In Iraq's cities, Western-style apartment buildings are common. Traditional Arab architecture—both rural and urban—often features buildings opening into private central courtyards, with blank walls facing the street.

Because of the hot climate in much of the country, traditional Iraqi Arab dress includes long, flowing robes offering protection from the sun. Arab women usually wear some type of head covering. Strongly devout Islamic women often cover their faces with veils. In modern cities, both men and women may wear Western-style clothing, although women rarely wear their hair loose and uncovered or wear short dresses or sleeveless clothing. Men often wear a head covering such as a skullcap or a loose headscarf called a *kaffiyeh,* held in place by a cord. Men sometimes combine Western and traditional clothing by wearing a sports jacket over a long robe.

Basic foods in the average Iraqi Arab diet include rice, beans, lentils, and chickpeas, which are often cooked into a paste and eaten with flat bread called pita. Dried or fresh fruits and sweet pastries are favorite desserts. Tea and thick, strong coffee are favorite drinks.

KURDS

The Kurds are the largest ethnic minority group in Iraq, making up about 15 to 20 percent of the population. They have their own culture and speak a language related to Persian. The name *Kurd* comes from the Persian word for "hero." Most Kurds belong to the Sunni branch of Islam. The Kurds live in the mountainous area in southwest Asia that is known as Kurdistan ("land of the Kurds"). Part of Kurdistan lies within the borders of Iraq, in the mountainous northern region. Kurdistan also extends into Turkey, Iran, Armenia, and Syria.

The Kurds were originally a nomadic people, following their herds of goats and sheep throughout the plains of Mesopotamia and the highlands of Iraq. The Kurdish people have existed for several thousand years, but they have never had their own government. Following World War I and the establishment of nation states, the Kurds were no longer free to follow their nomadic ways, as their land was divided up and given to other countries to rule. For decades, they have been attempting to establish their own independent Kurdish state. The nations of Turkey, Iraq, and Iran have opposed Kurdish independence, and Kurds have suffered harsh treatment at the hands of these governments.

The Kurds' strong sense of their own cultural identity is reflected in their colorful clothing. They shun traditional westernized clothing, such as suits or jeans and casual shirts. Dr. Vera Saeedpour, an authority on the Kurds, describes traditional Kurdish dress:

> A love of flowers is reflected in the Kurdish native garb, which is as colorful as their mountain flowers in spring. Men wear fringed turbans, baggy pants, matching jackets, and cummerbunds tied around their waists, most in earth tones. Women wear long dresses of brightly colored fabric and coats often of brocade [a rich cloth woven with a raised design] shot with silver or gold threads, baggy trousers, fancy vests, and headscarves. To see a Kurdish woman in her home setting is to see a riot of colors. [3]

Kurds love not only colorful clothing but also music, dance, and poetry. Kurds play music with a type of flute called a *zornah* and a drum called a *dohol*. Kurds were originally a tribal society and today are fiercely loyal to their tribe or village. This identification with a village or tribe is reflected in their dances; each region or village has its own special dance.

A dancing woman waves scarves in the red, gold, and green colors of the Kurdish flag. The Kurds make up the largest minority group in Iraq.

Traditionally, Kurdish loyalty to their tribes has led to serious infighting and hostility among groups. Even though Kurds have fought for an independent nation, some suggest that this tendency to fight among themselves would make it difficult for Kurds to establish a strong sense of national unity if granted an independent nation of their own.

MARSH ARABS

Far to the south of the Kurdish homeland live the Marsh Arabs, or Madan, an ancient people who make their home in the southern marshlands of Iraq. The Madan are descended from the ancient Sumerians and Babylonians who occupied the region thousands of years ago. In 1824, the Scottish traveler J. Baille Fraser described the Marsh Arab as the "stoutest, fairest and [most attractive] of all Arabs." He made special note of the women, whose "beauty, moreover, was not to be surpassed in the brilliant assemblies of civilised life!" [4]

Over the centuries some Persians and Bedouin intermarried with the Madan, but the Madan culture has remained rel-

The southern marshlands of Iraq are home to the Madan people, who build their houses and canoes from marsh reeds.

THE HOSPITALITY OF THE MARSH ARAB

In the 1920s, an author named Fulanain visited a Madan village in the watery marshes of Iraq. In his book *The Marsh Arab* he describes an ancient, traditional way of life that is fast disappearing:

> Hospitality among the Arabs of the desert has become a byword; yet it is not a [bit] less common among the humbler folk of the marsh, despised and wretched as they are. In the poorest household any small store of butter or other luxury which may have come its way is jealously reserved; and today, though meat is the rarest of luxuries, the Haji [headman] had killed a lamb in honour of his guest.

> Within the hut the women were busy over the fire. . . . Perfect peace brooded over the village as the warm afternoon drew to a close. The yellow and brown huts were sharply outlined against the deep blue of the sky. A group of buffaloes, their bodies submerged, showed motionless black heads above the surface of the water. The soft chatter of women inside Haji Rikkan's hut seemed hardly to ruffle the silence. . . .

> That evening several of the village elders were invited to partake of the Haji's hospitality. . . . Haji Rikkan's gnarled hand pulled [the roasted lamb] limb from limb; with his fingers he tore the tenderest pieces of meat from the back of the roasted lamb, and handed them to me with a great fistful of the stuffing. . . .

> The remnants of our food were left to reward the labours of the women who had cooked it. Not even the humblest Arab of the marsh would deign to eat with his wife. "We sleep in the same bed as our womenfolk," said the Haji once, "but eat with them? No, that were too great a disgrace."

atively unchanged for thousands of years, although now they practice Islam, like most Iraqi citizens. The uninviting marshlands kept the Madan isolated and kept unwanted visitors from interfering in Madan life and culture.

The traditional Madan way of life depends upon the reed plant. The reeds are plentiful and grow exceptionally large. The Madan travel in large reed canoes and build villages of arched reed huts. Large arches of reeds are used as the frame, which is supported by cross-beams made of reeds. The frame is then covered with layers of patterned reed mats to form the walls. The largest structure in the Madan village is the guest house, a cathedral-like arched hut called a *mudhif,* which is set upon a bank of woven reeds and furnished with carpets and cushions. (The Madan do not use furniture such as tables and chairs.) The practice of constructing the *mudhif* is as old

A Bedouin man wears traditional dress to keep cool in the desert. Nomadic Bedouin live throughout Iraq, Saudi Arabia, and Kuwait.

as the Madan civilization itself, and this craft of working with reeds has been passed down generation to generation for 5,000 years. Pictures of the *mudhif* have been found on seals dating from the Sumerian age.

The Madan traditionally keep water buffalo for milk and hides. They also use the water buffalo as work animals. Fish is an important part of the Madan diet. Traditionally, the Madan fish from their canoes with spears. In recent years, the Madan have begun to use nets to fish and to sell the surplus in the cities. The Madan also hunt the many waterfowl that inhabit the marshes.

The ancient Marsh Arab way of life is changing rapidly. Until the 1980s, about 100,000 Marsh Arabs inhabited 600,000 square miles in the marshes at the confluence of the Tigris and Euphrates rivers. The combination of the Iraqi war with Iran, the crisis over Kuwait, and the drying up of the marshlands has forced most of the people out. Many now live in refugee camps in Iran or elsewhere in Iraq.

BEDOUIN

Another small minority group in Iraq are the Bedouin. The name *Bedouin* comes from the Arabic word *bedu*, which means "inhabitant of the desert." Most Bedouin are Muslims and speak the Arabic language. The Bedouin are traditionally a nomadic people who wander seasonally with their herds of sheep, goats, and camels through desert areas of Iraq, Saudi Arabia, and Kuwait. A large neutral zone has been established between the borders of Iraq and Saudi Arabia so that the Bedouin may wander freely between these countries.

Dairy products, dates, and rice make up the main diet of the Bedouin. They trade dairy products and meat for manufactured goods such as pots and knives. The Bedouin live in large woven tents that are divided into two sections by a curtain. One section is for the men and the other for the women. Each tent houses a family. Bedouin have a tribal society, and the headman of the tribe is called the *sheik*. Bedouins are fiercely loyal to their families and their tribes, and they are extremely independent and proud. Any insult can lead to bloody feuds between tribes. Bedouins are also noted for

THE BEDOUIN WAY OF LIFE

For thousands of years, Bedouins have lived in the deserts of the Middle East, surviving and even thriving where many other people would die of thirst. Though their way of life is slowly fading away, replaced by technology, there are still traditional Bedouins living in Iraq and other countries.

Bedouins have a tribal society, and the leader of a Bedouin tribe is called a sheik. His authority is derived from heredity and the good faith of his people. Instead of signing an agreement, a Bedouin sheik has a stamp bearing his sign.

Bedouins often wear traditional clothing in the desert and out of it. The robe, or *jalabiyya,* is accompanied by headgear, which has two pieces: the cloth, or *kufiyya*, and rope, or *agal*. Married women wear an additional piece of clothing: a veil, or *asaba*.

Bedouins have specific customs for many things. Guests are treated to a ritual involving coffee when staying with a Bedouin. The first cup will be poured and tasted by the Bedouin, so the guest feels safe. The second will be poured and tasted by the guest, and the third will be drunk entirely by the guest.

Bedouins are masters of navigating in the desert; in fact, the word *Bedouin* comes from an Arabic word meaning "inhabitant of the desert." They use the stars to find their way, much like sailors before the invention of the compass. In addition, they can determine whether footprints belong to a man or woman.

Traditional Bedouins generally herd animals, usually sheep, goats, and camels. Much of their life is devoted to traveling the desert, seeking food and water for their animals. Because of this, territory is a valuable thing, and trespassing by members of one tribe on another's territory is a grave offense, which can be punished by death.

The Bedouin way of life can be harsh and difficult. However, many Bedouin still prefer the freedom of life in the desert.

their generosity. In the harsh and empty desert land that they travel, simply meeting another person was, and in some places still is, cause for extending courteous hospitality.

Although the Bedouin traditionally despise the agricultural life, many have abandoned their nomadic life and settled down. During the early and mid-1900s, Bedouins came increasingly under the control of newly formed nations. Many, however, continue to follow their traditional way of life, traveling the deserts in camel caravans, seeking fresh water and pasture for their animals. A traveler in the Iraqi deserts can still see the occasional Bedouin encampments of black tents or the train of camels slowly making their way single file across the parched land.

THE YAZIDIS

The Yazidis are a group of people who follow the religion of Yazidi, a unique religion that has elements of Islam, Christianity, Judaism, and several other religions. Iraq has the largest population of Yazidis, with about 500,000 of the estimated 700,000 Yazidis in the world. Almost all Yazidis speak Kurdish, though they remain separate from the rest of the Kurdish community.

Yazidis believe themselves to be the sole descendants from Adam. They believe that all other people are descended from Eve and are considered inferior. God is at the top in the Yazidi worldview, though he only created the world and does not actively take part in it. There are two important figures in Yazidi theology: Shaykh Adii, a god who was once a man and lived on Earth, and the fallen angel Malak Ta'us, who repented his sins. Malak Ta'us is represented as the Peacock Angel. According to Yazidi belief, Malak Ta'us filled seven jars of tears over 7,000 years, and these tears extinguished the fire in hell. Because of this, there is no hell in Yazidism. The Yazidis pray to Malak Ta'us twice a day, facing the sun. The most important ritual in Yazidism is a pilgrimage to the tomb of Shaykh Adii, which is north of the city of Mosul.

The Yazidis face persecution from both neighboring Sunni and Shiite Muslims, who view them as devil worshippers. This is in part because an alternative name for Malak Ta'us is Shaytan, the name for Satan in the Koran. They have also suffered along with their fellow Kurds in recent years at the hands of the Iraqi government.

OTHER GROUPS

Other ethnic minorities make up a small percentage of Iraq's population. Assyrians originally lived in the Zagros Mountains, and many fled to Iraq from Turkey during World War I. Assyrians speak a Syriac language and practice Christianity. Armenians were also originally Christian refugees from Turkey. Today a large community of Armenians lives in Baghdad and practices trade. Turkomen are descendants of Mongol invaders from Asia who ruled Iraq centuries ago. Most Turkomen live near the cities of Mosul and Kirkuk.

Northwestern Iraq is home to a group called the Yazidis. They are a religious people who consider both the Bible and the Koran as holy books. They speak a form of Kurdish but use Arabic in their religious practices. The emblem of the Yazidis is the Peacock Angel.

Over thousands of years, the land that is now Iraq has been home to a variety of ethnic groups. Some groups of people who now inhabit Iraq are relative newcomers to this ancient land. Others, such as the Madan and the Kurds, have inhabited the land for thousands of years. These ancient groups contributed to the development of the world's earliest civilization.

3

THE CRADLE OF CIVILIZATION

One of the most dramatic changes in the history of humanity took place when human beings gave up hunting and gathering and settled down in villages to farm and raise animals. One of the first places that human beings made this change was in Mesopotamia. Today the modern nation of Iraq occupies this land that has been home to the first and some of the most impressive civilizations the world has known.

SUMER—MESOPOTAMIA'S FIRST CIVILIZATION

Some 5,000 years ago, a group of people known as the Sumerians who lived along the Tigris and Euphrates rivers began building the world's first civilization. The rich farm lands of Mesopotamia allowed Sumerian farmers to grow more than enough food to feed themselves. They began trading their surplus crops with other communities. Gradually Mesopotamia became a trading center, and the small market towns grew into thriving cities. Irrigation was essential to agriculture in the region. To build and maintain the irrigation systems, people had to organize themselves and work together. This organization of society eventually led to the development of the first true cities, which appeared about 3500 B.C.

The ancient Sumerians were the first to develop the basic tools of civilization. The most important development of ancient Sumer was a system of writing. As trade expanded, Sumerians needed a method of keeping track of their goods. Pictographs, or pictures that stood for whole words, were inscribed on wet clay tablets in a system known as cuneiform. Gradually, writing became more complex, and people began using writing to record events and stories and to pass on information from one generation to the next. This development in writing marked the beginning of the historical period, as people for the first time began keeping records of important events. Great libraries were established by 2700 B.C.

Other inventions of the Sumerians included the plow, which was important in advancing the development of agriculture. The first plow was just a tree branch pulled by one person and pushed by another. Later, the Sumerians invented a copper plow that could be pulled by oxen, and later a bronze plow. Sumerians also established the world's first formal school, known as the *edubba.* Only boys (not girls) from wealthy families attended the *edubba,* where students learned reading, writing, and arithmetic. Discipline was strict, and students could be beaten for minor offenses.

THE HOUSE OF TABLETS

Life at the *edubba,* or "house of tablets," was difficult for students. In this story—one of several versions told by the Sumerians—a young boy has difficulty in school but manages to overcome his obstacles:

> Pupil, where have you been all this time? At the house of tablets. What did you do there? I read the clay tablet and ate. I covered my tablet right to the edge with writing. When school was over, I went straight home and recited to my father what I had learned. I read out to him what I had written and he was satisfied. Next morning I had to get up early. I went to my mother and said to her: "Give me something to eat, for I have to go to school." She then took two rolls from the oven and she sat by me as I drank. I ran off with my lunch bread. But the school janitor said: "You are far too late." Then I was afraid and my heart began to thump. I went to the teacher and he said: "Go to your place!" He looked at my tablet and was angry and he beat me.

The pupil then tries to gain the favor of his teacher by asking his father to invite the teacher home. The father gives the teacher gifts—clothing, a gold ring, and some money. The teacher is appeased and tells the pupil:

> Boy, because you have paid heed to my words and did not ignore them, you may attain the peak of the scribe's art and master it entirely. You will become the leader of your brothers and the captain of your friends, you will be the best among the pupils. You have done your school tasks well. You are now a man of knowledge.

Sumerian civilization was based on independent city-states—centers that included the city and its surrounding land. Lagash, one of the largest city-states, had a population of nearly 35,000. It covered 1800 square miles. Some other important city-states were Erech, Kish, and Ur, whose populations were in the thousands. (The city of Ur is mentioned in the Bible as the place from which Abraham departed to establish a new nation in the land of Canaan.) Each city-state had a patron god and goddess and was originally ruled by a priest-king. To honor their gods, the Sumerians built temples in the form of large stepped pyramids called *ziggurats*. Ziggurat means "mountain of gods." Ziggurats eventually became the center of administration for the city-state.

The priestly class and nobles occupied the top of ancient Sumerian society. A little lower were the merchants and scholars, and below them the craftspeople and artisans. At the bottom of society were the peasants and the slaves taken in warfare.

This ancient mask from about 2250 B.C. depicts the Akkadian ruler Sargon the Great who established the first true empire in Mesopotamia.

GROWTH OF CIVILIZATION

Over the centuries, some city-states became more powerful than others. About 2330 B.C., the Akkadian people conquered all of the territory of Sumer and extended its rule. Although the Akkadians also lived in Mesopotamia, they were different from the Sumerians. They spoke a Semitic language related to modern Hebrew and Arabic. The most famous Akkadian ruler was Sargon the Great, who extended his rule into parts of what are today Turkey, Syria, and Iran, establishing a central authority and the first great empire in Mesopotamia. Although the Akkadian empire was short-lived, lasting only about 100 years, it paved the way for later empires. Later rulers tried to follow Sargon's example of establishing a unified "greater Mesopotamia" under one central ruler.

Following the fall of the Akkadians, there was a renewal of Sumerian civilization. But Mesopotamia, with its rich cities and fertile

THE EPIC OF GILGAMESH

One of the oldest stories from Mesopotamia is *The Epic of Gilgamesh*, which dates from between 1500 and 2500 B.C. Gilgamesh was the tyrant king of Uruk, a city on the Euphrates River in northern Iraq. This story has many parallels with other ancient texts. According to the translation of Gilgamesh by N.K. Sandars, one of these is the earliest reference to the great flood (perhaps a precursor to the biblical tale of Noah), in which Utnapishtim, "the great king of the world before the flood," was the only mortal, with his wife, to survive.

At the beginning of the story, "Gilgamesh is the epitome of a bad ruler," and the Sumerian gods create a man-beast, Enkidu, to punish him. When the two finally meet, they fight,

> . . . holding each other like bulls. They broke the doorposts and the walls shook, they snorted like bulls locked together. . . . Gilgamesh bent his knee with his foot planted on the ground and with a turn Enkidu was thrown. Then immediately his fury died. When Enkidu was thrown he said to Gilgamesh, "There is not another like you in the world. Nunsun, who is as strong as a wild ox in the byre, she was the mother who bore you, and now you are raised above all men, and Enlil has given you the kingship, for your strength surpasses the strength of me." So Enkidu and Gilgamesh embraced and their friendship was sealed.

After this, the two have many adventures. Enkidu dies after the two offend the goddess Ishtar, and Gilgamesh is distraught. His final adventures take him on a journey to find the secret of immortality, and the story ends with his return to Uruk.

Gilgamesh is unique in its antiquity. It was composed over an entire millennium, and tablets containing passages from it have been found in every language that was written in cuneiform. For comparison, this story predates literate civilization in Europe by over a thousand years.

---

lands, was still tempting to the Semitic tribes on the fringes of the region. (Semites are people who speak a Semitic language such as Hebrew or Arabic. Ancient Assyrians, Babylonians, Canaanites, and Hebrews were Semites.) The Amorites, semi-nomadic herders, were feared raiders who posed a serious threat to Sumer. They were also described by the Sumerians as a savage people who ate raw meat, left their dead unburied, and lived outside without shelter. Not all Amorites were raiders, however. Some settled into life in Sumer, taking on the culture and way of life.

Weakness from within and raiders from without led to the final decline and destruction of the kingdom of Ur in 2006 B.C.

The city of Ur suffered severely at the hands of the invaders. The final destruction of Ur is recorded in a long poem by an unknown Sumerian author, the *Lamentation over the Destruction of Ur*, which reads in part:

> How, O Sumer, are thy mighty fallen!
> The holy king is banished from his temple.
> The temple itself is destroyed, the city demolished.
> The leaders of the nation have been carried off into captivity.
> A whole empire has been overthrown by the will of the gods. [5]

The "holy king" is Ibi-Sin, the last of the great kings of Ur. A long period of confusion followed the fall of Ur.

BABYLONIA

The Semitic-speaking Amorites finally succeeded in subjugating the Sumerian-Akkadians. An important turning point in the history of the region came when the Amorites established a new state about 2000 B.C. The descendants of the Amorites, who became known as Babylonians, set up another empire in Mesopotamia, with the city of Babylon as its capital. Babylon was the grandest city of the ancient world, admired by the Romans as "the greatest city the sun ever beheld." [6] Babylonia flourished for nearly two thousand years, until it was conquered by Alexander the Great in 331 B.C.

Babylonian culture was much like that of the Sumerians. The Babylonians were farmers and traders. They kept animals and used cotton and wool textiles. Priests, nobles, and wealthy traders made up the upper class. Merchants, clerks, and craftspeople were in the middle class. At the bottom were peasant farmers and slaves. They also adopted many religious beliefs of the Sumerians. Each city had its own god as protector.

The first important Babylonian king was Hammurabi, who came to power about 1792 B.C. Hammurabi conquered most of Mesopotamia and brought it under his rule. However, he is most noted for his establishment of a code of laws, known as the Code of Hammurabi. This code included laws on personal property, real estate, injuries, the family, trade and business, and labor. The code contained many principles of the ancient law of "an eye for an eye." For example, if a builder built a house that later collapsed, killing the owner, then the builder would be put to death. However, Hammurabi also introduced the idea of having the accused pay fines to the injured party, rather than being punished by death or mutilation. Scholars suggest that the Code of Hammurabi encouraged the much later development of a formal legal system with courts and judges.

Hammurabi had his laws inscribed on stele (stone slabs) or cylinders and spread throughout his kingdom. At the end of the code of laws, Hammurabi has these words:

> In my bosom I carried the people of the land of Sumer and Akkad. . . . In my wisdom I restrained them, that the strong might not oppress the weak, and that they should give justice to the orphan and the widow.[7]

Following Hammurabi's rule, however, Babylonia began to decline. Revolts in the south and invasions from the north weakened the empire, and in 1595 B.C. Babylon was overrun by a nomadic tribe known as the Hittites. This ended the Hammurabi dynasty and began a period of disorder in which other tribes from the north attacked and took over the region. A new dynasty emerged, founded by the conquering tribe, the Kassites. The conquerors adopted Babylonian culture and ruled the region for about 600 years.

The Stele of Hammurabi depicts Babylonian king Hammurabi approaching Shamash, the God of Justice (seated). The stone stele is inscribed with the legal Code of Hammurabi.

ASSYRIA

Along the upper Tigris River, in the northern part of what is now Iraq, lay the land of the Assyrians, another Semitic people. The Assyrians were a warlike people and used their well-organized armies to conquer neighboring people and extend their empire.

The civilization of the Assyrians (literally the "children of Ashur") was centered around the cities of Ashur, Erbil, Nimrud, and Nineveh. While the Kassites were ruling Babylon, the Assyrian kings of the 800s B.C. were building an empire. The empire reached its height during the reign of Ashurnasirpal II (883–859 B.C.), who conquered parts of Babylonia, Arabia, and what are now Egypt, Jordan, Israel, and Syria.

The Assyrians were fierce fighters and ruthless conquerors and were generally hated

throughout the Mesopotamian and the Middle Eastern regions where they extended their influence. One of the Assyrian kings, Tiglath-Pileser I, left this inscription on stone:

> In my fierce valour I marched against the people of Qummuh, conquered their cities, carried off their booty, their goods and their property without reckoning, and burned their cities with fire—destroyed and devastated them. . . . The people of Adansh left their mountains and embraced my feet. I imposed taxes upon them.[8]

Perhaps the most ruthless was Sennacherib (705–681 B.C.), who supposedly sacked 89 cities and captured 208,000 prisoners. He then went on to attack the city of Babylon, which was resisting Assyrian control, and slaughtered all of its inhabitants, until the corpses were piled high in the streets. Despite his ruthlessness, it was Sennacherib who built the Assyrian capital of Nineveh into a magnificent city. He laid out streets and squares, built a large palace, filling it with sculpture looted in his many conquests. At its height, Nineveh was home to 300,000 people.

By the mid-600s B.C., the Assyrian empire was beginning to fall apart. Ashurbanipal (669–626 B.C.) was the last of the notable Assyrian kings. He built a great library at Nineveh, which included the ancient Sumerian masterpieces *The Epic of Gilgamesh* and *The Epic of Creation*, which have given modern scholars insight into the earliest Mesopotamian civilization. In 612 B.C., not long after the death of Ashurbanipal, the Assyrian empire fell before the onslaught of the Babylonian forces and their allies. The final destruction of Nineveh is the subject of the Old Testament Book of Nahum, which reads in part:

> And it shall come to pass, that all they that look upon thee shall flee from thee, and say, Nineveh is laid waste: who will bemoan her? . . . Thy Shepherds slumber, O king of Assyria: thy nobles shall dwell in the dust: thy people is scattered upon the mountains, and no man gathereth them. There is no healing of thy bruises; thy wound is grievous: all that hear the [clamor] of thee shall clap the hands over thee: for upon whom hath not thy wickedness passed continually? (Nahum 3:7, 17–19)

THE NEW BABYLON

The last of the ancient Mesopotamian kingdoms was the shortest lived—only 67 years—but one of the most famous. One of the tribes that helped in the destruction of the Assyrian empire was the Chaldeans. This tribe, which had been

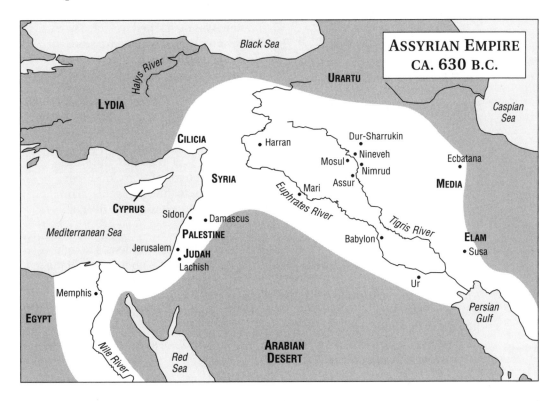

THE HANGING GARDENS OF BABYLON

The legendary Hanging Gardens of Babylon are considered one of the Seven Wonders of the Ancient World. Though they have been written about for millennia, archaeologists have yet to verify that they actually existed.

The earliest accounts of the gardens available (written hundreds of years after they were supposedly built) generally agree on most details. The gardens were built by King Nebuchadnezzar II, who ruled Babylon from approximately 602 to 562 B.C. Nebuchadnezzar built the gardens to cheer up his favorite wife, Amytis, who was from the mountainous region of Media (modern Azerbaijan and northern Iran). She missed her lush, terraced homeland. Mesopotamia was flat and dreary in comparison.

The gardens were planted on a terraced ziggurat (pyramid) that simulated a mountain. The gardens probably did not actually hang, though plants may have dangled over the terraces. An advanced irrigation system was developed in such a way that water was lifted by slave labor from the Euphrates River to the top of the pyramid and ran down its slopes like mountain streams, feeding all the plants. According to the ancient historian Diodorus Siculus:

Archaeologists do not know if the Hanging Gardens of Babylon ever really existed.

> The approach to the Garden sloped like a hillside and the several parts of the structure rose from one another tier on tier. . . . On all this, the earth had been piled . . . and was thickly planted with trees of every kind that, by their great size and other charm, gave pleasure to the beholder. . . . The water machines [raised] the water in great abundance from the river, although no one outside could see it.

There is speculation about the existence of the Hanging Gardens. Though Herodotus wrote in detail about Babylon in 450 B.C., there is no mention of the gardens until later accounts, after Alexander the Great's conquest of Persia. Archaeologists have found a likely structure in the ancient ruin of the city, but the Greek historian Strabo's account places the gardens next to the Euphrates River, and this building is far from there.

Whether they existed or not, the Hanging Gardens have secured their place in legend as a wonder of the world.

pushing the borders of southern Babylonia for several centuries, finally took control of Babylon itself. The most famous king of this period was Nebuchadnezzar (602–562 B.C.). Nebuchadnezzar was a famous builder, who erected a new capital on the site of the old Babylon. He copied many of the building plans from the city of Nineveh and made an even grander city. According to tradition, one of his most memorable structures was the Hanging Gardens of Babylon, one of the Seven Wonders of the Ancient World.

Nebuchadnezzar wished to be remembered as a builder and as "the wise, the reverent, the worshipper of the great gods."[9] However, he is more often remembered for his capture of Jerusalem in 597 B.C., during which he took the people of Jerusalem into slavery "by the waters of Babylon" (that is, by the system of canals from the Euphrates River that surrounded the city and was maintained by slaves). The ruins of Babylon today (which are being rebuilt by the current Iraqi leader, Saddam Hussein) are from this new Babylon that was built by Nebuchadnezzar. Nothing remains of King Hammurabi's old city of Babylon.

LATER CONQUERORS

Through the following centuries, Mesopotamia would be a battleground and a crossroads for foreign conquerors and rulers from the east and from the west. In 539 B.C., Cyrus the Great of Persia (now Iran) led his army into Babylonia, laying

In this painting, Alexander the Great lies on his deathbed in the city of Babylon. Alexander brought Greek rule to Babylonia in 331 B.C.

siege to the city of Babylon and defeating its defenders. For the next 200 years Babylonia was part of the Persian Empire.

In 331 B.C., Alexander the Great of Macedonia invaded Babylonia, defeating the Persians and bringing Greek rule. Alexander, one of the greatest generals in history, conquered Persia and what is modern Afghanistan, crossing into India. There he built a fleet of ships to sail down the Indus River and back to Babylon via the Persian Gulf. Alexander died in the city of Babylon in 323 B.C. Alexander's great empire was split, and his cavalry general Seleucis took over the portion of Alexander's conquests that is now modern Iraq. Seleucis built a new capital, Seleucia, on the Tigris River, twenty miles from Babylon. Seleucid domination lasted 175 years, but the Greek cultural influence in the region continued for several centuries.

Following the Seleucids, the Parthians, a warlike group from Persia, conquered the region in about 200 B.C. The Parthians maintained power for 400 years, despite attempts by the Romans to conquer them.

The Parthians fell at last to the Sassanian Persians, or Sassanids. The most famous Sassanid king was Chosroes, who built the new capital city of Ctesiphon. The age of Chosroes is remembered as a kind of golden age. In his magnificent palace of Sapor, the great Arch of Chosroes—a wide brick arch—soared 120 feet over the banqueting hall. Its remains can still be seen today in Ctesiphon, near modern Baghdad. Chosroes encouraged poetry, philosophy, and translations of Greek and Indian works. The game of chess originated under Chosroes and passed to the Western world. He maintained the ancient irrigation canals throughout his domain. The long period of Sassanid rule (some 400 years) was the last foreign rule before the next great epoch in Iraqi history.

THE COMING OF ARABS AND ISLAM

For 4,000 years, ancient Mesopotamia was the site of the rise and fall of empires, of dramatic cultural achievements, and of the human suffering that comes with the turbulence of warfare and tyrannical rulers. Then in about 570 A.D. a man was born whose teachings and whose followers would dramatically change the course of history in Mesopotamia and far beyond: the prophet Muhammad. Muhammad was born in the city of Mecca in what is now Saudi Arabia. When he was about

40 years old, he experienced what his followers believe were visions sent by the "one true
God." The Muslim holy book, the Koran, is
the record of what his followers believe are
the words of God as revealed to Muhammad.
The religion he established is called Islam.
The message of Islam was that all people
should turn away from the many gods and
goddesses they had been worshipping and
submit themselves to the one God, Allah.

Following Muhammad's death in 632, the
Arab Muslims (followers of Islam) rode out of
their home in the deserts of Arabia and set
out to spread their religion. They were phe-
nomenally successful, and by 637, the Muslims had taken the city of Ctesiphon, capital
of the Sassanids. Just twenty-four years after
Muhammad's death, his fourth successor, or
caliph, ruled a vast Arab Islamic empire from
what is now Tunis in Africa to Afghanistan.

A Victorian-era drawing portrays Islam's prophet, Muhammad. Islam teaches that Muhammad is God's intermediary.

Muhammad has been depicted in art over the centuries,
although images of him often do not show his facial features
because it is considered disrespectful in some Islamic countries.

In A.D. 762, the Abbasid dynasty of caliphs (named after
Muhammad's uncle Abbas) established their capital at Baghdad. The caliph combined both spiritual authority and kingly
rule. At its height under the Abbasids, the city of Baghdad was
home to nearly a million people and was as grand as ancient
Babylon. Situated on the west bank of the Tigris River, it was a
round city, with an outer ring of walls and two inner rings of
walls. At the city's center was a grand mosque (the Muslim
house of worship), larger than any cathedral of Europe. The
city soon became the center of a large Arab empire that included all of the Arabian Peninsula and the Middle East and
stretched from Central Asia westward along North Africa to include most of Spain and Portugal. This vast empire was held
together by Arabic, the official language of the empire, and Islam, the official religion. The Abbasid culture combined elements of Persian literature, music, and architecture. The
Abbasid empire, renowned for learning and the arts, achieved
a brilliant civilization, reflecting ideas from Greece, Rome, and

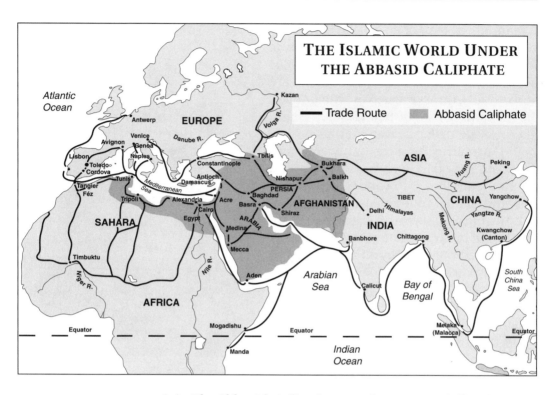

THE ISLAMIC WORLD UNDER THE ABBASID CALIPHATE

Asia. The Abbasid civilization was the greatest civilization west of China and surpassed Western Europe for centuries.

Abbasid rule lasted 500 years, ten times as long as the modern state of Iraq has lasted. The empire reached its height under the caliph Harun al-Rashid (A.D. 786–809), who is mentioned in the collection of tales popularly known as *One Thousand and One Nights*. The empire gradually declined, with the caliphs becoming more figureheads than rulers. Then in 1258, the land that is now Iraq began a dark and terrible period of decay.

MONGOLS AND OTTOMANS

In the thirteenth century, nomadic Mongol raiders from the steppes of Asia terrorized much of the civilized world, from Europe to the Middle East. Ruthless and destructive, the Mongol conqueror Genghis Khan declared that "All cities must be razed, so that the world may once again become a great steppe [a semiarid grass-covered plain] in which Mongol mothers will suckle free and happy children." [10] The Mongols nearly succeeded in wiping out civilization from the region of Mesopotamia. In 1258, Mongols invaded and sacked

Baghdad, wiping out the Abbasid dynasty and Arab rule. The Arab chronicler Ibn al-Athir describes the great catastrophe brought by the Mongols:

> To whom, indeed, can it be easy to write the death-blow of Islam and the Muslims. . . . This thing involves the description of the greatest catastrophe and the most dire

THE GOLDEN AGE OF ISLAM

During the eighth and ninth centuries, while Europe was living through the Dark Ages, the Islamic world was in a golden age. While many European rulers were unable to read, Arab scholars were constructing great works of mathematics, science, and philosophy.

In the vast Islamic empire, Arabic became the language of scholarship, just as Latin had been in the Roman Empire. Arab scholars preserved the works of ancient Greece. They studied the ideas of the philosophers Aristotle and Plato, the ideas of the mathematician Euclid, and the medical learning of Galen. Greek texts were translated into Arabic at Baghdad's great library, the House of Wisdom. Arab scholars eventually reintroduced this classical learning to Europe.

In addition to preserving the learning of ancient Greece, the Arab world introduced its own discoveries and inventions. In science, some of their contributions include the first chemical laboratories, in which Islamic chemists, in an attempt to turn ordinary metals into gold, found how to separate chemical compounds from one another. The medical scholar Avicenna (980–1037) wrote a five-volume encyclopedia of medicine that was used by European doctors for six centuries. The astrolabe, an instrument used in astronomy and first used by the Greeks, was improved by Islamic astronomers as an effective tool for navigation.

In mathematics, the mathematician Al-Khowarizmi (for whom the term "algorithm" is named) developed the mathematical technique he called *al-jabr* (which we call algebra). Arab mathematicians adopted a number system that is based on sets of ten and includes a zero, which is known today as Arabic numerals. (Before this was introduced to Europe, the ancient Roman system was still in place. Imagine, instead of writing 34 + 29 = 63, writing XXXIV + XXIX = LXIII.) Without the Arabic system of numbers, higher math would be far too cumbersome to make sense.

calamity . . . which befell all men generally, and the Muslims in particular. . . . These [Mongols] spared none, slaying women and men and children, ripping open pregnant women and killing unborn babies.[11]

It is estimated that about 800,000 people were killed over several days in Baghdad. The destruction was nearly complete. The Mongols destroyed much of the irrigation system, without which the people could not grow crops. Although Baghdad continued to exist, what was left of the irrigation systems fell into decay, and the surrounding countryside became a near wasteland. Baghdad was no longer the thriving center of trade it had been for centuries. As the central authority in Baghdad failed, nomadic tribes began to invade the settled areas throughout the region. Baghdad and the people of Mesopotamia suffered for centuries. In 1401, Baghdad was once again invaded by Mongols, led by Tamerlane, who repeated the horrific destruction.

Beginning in the 1300s, Muslims in what is now Turkey began to develop an empire. Known as the Ottomans (from the founder of the dynasty Osman I, or in Arabic Uthman), these Muslim Turks eventually extended their empire into the Mid-

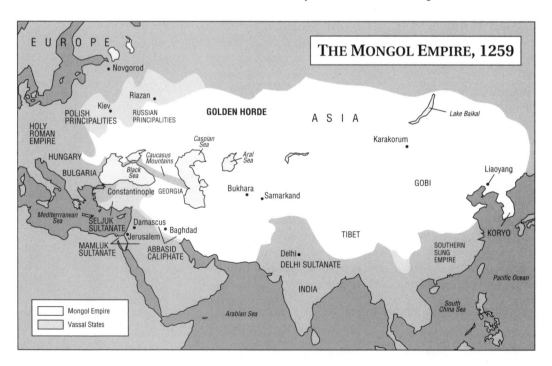

dle East. Led by the Ottoman conqueror, Suleyman the Magnificent, the Turks captured Baghdad and conquered Mesopotamia
in 1534. The Ottomans ruled Mesopotamia until 1918, except for
brief periods of Persian control.

Far from the Ottoman capital of Constantinople (now Istan-
bul) and the authority of Turkish administrators, Mesopotamia
remained a backwater, underdeveloped and poorly governed.
Finally in 1869, as a result of reform in the Ottoman government, a new governor was sent to the region. The region began
to come alive once again under the reforms, which included
emphasis on education and land reform. New schools—free
to all boys (no girls received education)—taught mathematics,
geography, science, and foreign languages. Development continued into the first decade of the twentieth century. But as the
Ottoman Empire declined, Mesopotamia came under the influence of yet other foreign powers—the Western nations.

4

WESTERN INFLUENCE AND THE MODERN WORLD

During the 1500s and 1600s the Ottoman Empire was one of the most powerful empires in the world. But the Ottomans began a slow decline in the 1700s, as the nations of Europe began to grow in power. Europeans were interested in expanding their commercial interests and areas of influence and building empires. They turned their attention to the East, where the weakening Ottoman Empire and lack of strong central governments offered the opportunity for their expansionist ambitions. The region of Mesopotamia became important for its resources, as well as its location. Britain in particular exerted an enormous influence in the region. It was Britain that drew the boundaries of the Iraqi nation, decided its form of government, and installed the first Iraqi king.

IMPACT OF THE WEST

By the 1800s Britain controlled India and had become interested in the Persian Gulf area—then under Ottoman rule—to protect its trade routes between Europe and India. By the beginning of World War I in 1914, Britain had another interest in the region—the oil of Mesopotamia. In the 1840s, it had been discovered that kerosene could be distilled from oil and used for lighting lamps. (In the United States, whale oil had been the main source of lamp oil up to that time.) Other uses for oil were found. By the early 1900s, oil was being refined for use as fuel in motor vehicles, and the demand for oil continued to grow dramatically.

There had long been stories about "black oily substances" in Arabic literature. Bitumen, a tarlike substance used for waterproofing, had been used for centuries in the Middle East. Oil was discovered in Egypt in 1869, and later in Persia,

Iraq, and Kuwait. The growing need for oil ensured that the Middle East would be a focus for the Western industrialized nations.

When World War I began, the Ottoman Empire, based in Turkey, supported Germany and declared war against Britain and its allies. Britain invaded what is now Iraq and eventually captured Baghdad, removing it from Ottoman rule. The British promised the people that they would have some control over their own land. The war was an important turning point for the entire region of the Middle East. Arabs were promised their own Arab nation in return for revolting against the Ottomans. A single, independent Arab state was to be made up of what are now Syria, Lebanon, Iraq, Transjordan (modern Jordan), and Palestine (modern Israel).

THE NEW NATION OF IRAQ

The Arabs were soon disappointed, however. When the war was over, the modern nations of the Middle East were set up with new boundaries and placed under British and French mandates by the League of Nations. (The League of Nations was an association of nations formed at the end of World War I, the purpose of which was to maintain peace in the world.) Britain controlled the newly formed nation of Iraq, as well as the areas of Palestine and Transjordan. France was given Syria and Lebanon.

The arrangement was a bitter blow to Arab people throughout the region, who thought they had been promised independence. The people of the region had been under foreign control since the 1200s. They saw the mandate as just another type of foreign control. The only redeeming feature of the mandate was that the mandate powers (Britain and France) were obligated to train the people for independence. But the people of Iraq revolted against what they saw as their new masters, and Iraq was in turmoil for several months.

Forging the diverse people of Iraq into a united independent nation would not be easy. When the boundaries of Middle Eastern states were being drawn, the Europeans ignored the differences in ethnic groups and social systems of the people who lived there. In southern Iraq, the city of Basra sits on the Shatt al-Arab River, over 300 miles from the capital of Baghdad. Most of the people in the south belonged to the Shia branch of Islam. Between Basra and Baghdad lay the marshes, home of the Madan. In central Iraq, many of the people belonged to the Sunni branch of Islam. In the mountainous north, the area around the city of Mosul is home to a large population of non-Arab Kurds, who hoped to have an independent nation of their own. In rural areas, people traditionally considered the authority to be the village headman or tribal sheikh. They felt little or no loyalty to a central ruler hundreds of miles away.

The government that the British decided to install was a monarchy, modeled after their own government. But they needed a monarch they could control and who would be acceptable to all of the people. The man chosen was Faisal, an Arab leader from a royal family. His father had been ruler of the city of Mecca under the Ottomans. Faisal belonged to the Hashemite dynasty, descendants of the prophet Muhammad. Faisal had led Arab forces against the Ottomans during the war. At the end of World War I, Faisal had marched triumphantly into the city of Damascus in Syria, as Arab leaders proclaimed him king of Syria, the new independent Arab state. His triumph was short-lived when the French deposed him and took over Syria as their mandate, leaving King Faisal without a throne. He seemed by the British to be the most likely candidate for king of Iraq.

FROM MONARCHY TO REPUBLIC

Even though Faisal was an outsider, he was a popular ruler, reigning for 12 years. During that time, improvements were made in roads and irrigation canals. Oil was discovered in 1927, and the petroleum industry was developed. Income from oil gave the Iraqi economy a boost. However, Iraq remained a British mandate, and the British made sure that all government policies were favorable to their country.

In 1929 Britain notified Iraq that the mandate would end in 1932 and Iraq would become an independent nation, after a treaty was negotiated between Iraq and Britain. The new treaty was signed on June 30, 1930, and, in 1932, after more than a decade under the British mandate, Iraq became an independent state and a member of the League of Nations. However, according to the treaty between Iraq and Britain, Britain still maintained the right to use Iraqi air bases, roads, and harbors and to station troops in Iraq if necessary. This arrangement was not what the people considered true independence, and they voiced their opposition through strikes and demonstrations. Government power was held by a small group of elites, however, and despite the opposition of the people, Britain maintained its influence.

Despite more than ten years of preparation, it was questionable whether Iraq was ready for independence. As King Faisal said, "In Iraq there is still no Iraqi people but unimaginable masses of human beings, lacking any patriotic ideal, connected by no common tie, prone to anarchy and always ready to rise against any government whatsoever." [12]

In 1933, King Faisal died and was succeeded by his son King Ghazi. Ghazi was a reckless twenty-one-year-old who liked to drive fast cars. At the time Ghazi took the throne, the Iraqi national army was growing in power and becoming deeply involved in politics. In 1936 the military staged a *coup d'état* (a takeover of the government by force). Although the army left Ghazi as king, they controlled the government. Another military coup took place in 1938, in which General Nuri al-Said seized power. Nuri had no intention of establishing a democratic state or a free press. He was conservative and strongly pro-British, and the British continued to maintain their influence in Iraq. This military takeover set the pattern of politics in Iraq for the next forty years, until the time that Saddam Hussein took over as dictator.

After a short-lived stint as king of Syria, King Faisal became Iraq's leader, ruling until his death in 1933.

In 1939 King Ghazi was killed in a car crash. He left as his successor his four-year-old son, who became known as Faisal II. Ghazi's uncle Abdul Ilah was appointed as crown prince to rule for the young boy until he became old enough to rule. For almost two decades, Iraq was governed by a small, elite pro-British group. The elite ruling group was all Sunni Muslims, while the majority of the Iraqi people belonged to the Shia branch of Islam, a fact much resented by the people. The two most powerful figures in the government remained Crown Prince Abdul Illah and Nuri al-Said, who acted as prime minister no less than fourteen times between 1930 and 1958. During World War II, opposition pro-German military leaders attempted to take over the government, but the British quickly put down the coup and restored the government of Nuri al-Said. Despite the calls for reform and more openness in government, Nuri al-Said banned political parties, causing even more unrest.

Many Iraqis were also opposed to the government's ties to Western nations because those nations supported the state of Israel. Iraqi Arabs, like many Arabs throughout the Middle East, were angry that the Jews had been given land to establish a state. They believed the land occupied by Israel had been promised to the Palestinian Arabs to form an independent state of Palestine. Iraqis saw this as another promise broken by Western powers.

REVOLUTION AND REPUBLIC

Finally on July 14, 1958, officers of the Iraqi army overthrew the elite Iraqi government. Nuri al-Said, Crown Prince Abdul Ilah, and King Faisal II were all murdered. General Abdul Karim Kassem became prime minister and commander in chief. Once the takeover was secure, Kassem made a radio broadcast to the people:

> The affairs of this country must be entrusted to a government [coming from] the people and working under its inspiration. This can only be achieved by the formation of a popular republic to uphold complete Iraqi unity, to bind itself with bonds of fraternity with Arab and Muslim countries. . . . This national government shall be known from now on by the name of the Iraqi Republic. [13]

Kassem found that ruling Iraq was no easier for him than it had been for any of his predecessors. The social, political, and religious factions that had been suppressed under Nuri al-

Abdul Karim Kassem works in his office in 1958. Kassem became Iraqi prime minister following a coup by the Iraqi army.

THE COMING OF THE BAATH PARTY

The word *Baath* is Arabic for "resurrection." Originally, the Baath Party was known as *al-Hizb al-Baath al-Arabi* ("Party of the Arab Resurrection"). The mission of the party was to unite all of the Arab peoples of the Middle East into one Arab nation. Michael Aflaq, a Syrian Arab, originally founded the party in the 1940s. According to Aflaq,

> The party of the Arab Baath is a socialist party. It believes that the economic wealth of the fatherland belongs to the Arab nation. Socialism arises from the depths of Arab nationalism. It makes up the ideal social order that will allow the Arab people to realize their possibilities, to enable their genius to flourish, and to ensure for the Arab nation constant progress.

The idea of pan-Arabism, or the uniting of all Arabs into a single nation, seemed more remote, as Arab nations became independent after World War II. But in Iraq, the Baath Party gained a foothold when Michael Aflaq himself moved from Syria to Baghdad. When the Baath General Ahmad Hasan al-Bakr came to power, Michael Aflaq was given an important post, which he kept until his death in 1989. Because of Aflaq's presence, the Iraqi Baath Party has claimed to be the official representative for all Arabs.

Said's government now reemerged and began their old struggle for power. Groups such as the Baath Party supported Iraq's joining Egyptian president Gamal Abdel Nasser's drive for a union of all Arab countries, an idea called Pan-Arabism. Iraqi Communists, along with the Kassem government, opposed this pan-Arab movement, hoping for a truly independent state. Following the revolt, the Kassem government turned on the communists and attempted to suppress them. In the north, the Kurds once again began agitating for their own independent nation. Various groups attempted unsuccessfully to overthrow Kassem between 1958 and 1963.

Finally, in 1961 Kassem made a fatal mistake. Iraq laid claim to the tiny neighboring country of Kuwait. Kassem found that he had no support—either internationally or from his own people—for this action. Two years later Kassem was assassinated. His place was taken by Colonel Abdul Salam Arif and another group of army officers and supporters of the

Iraqi leaders (from left to right) Deputy Premier Hardan Tikriti, President Ahmad Hasan al-Bakr, and Chief of Staff Hammad Chehab salute at a military parade in 1969.

Baath political party. Among the group was a young officer named Saddam Hussein.

Over the next few years, one or another of various factions claimed power. During this period, important development projects such as new hospitals, schools, and roads were neglected. The country was in turmoil, with uprisings, political repression, and executions of political opponents with each new government. In 1966 Arif died in a helicopter crash. His brother took his place but was exiled in 1968, following a coup by the Baath Party. Baath Party supporter General Ahmad Hasan al-Bakr took control, with yet another round of political repression or execution of opponents. Although al-Bakr was named president of the republic, no cabinet ministers were appointed and no parliamentary government was established. Instead, power was placed in a seven-man Revolutionary Command Council (RCC). (One member of the RCC was Saddam Hussein.) The Baath Party had finally achieved power and would hold onto it into the twenty-first century.

When General Ahmad Hasan al-Bakr took over the government of Iraq, he brought the first stability the country had known for years. An important change was the nationalization (taking under government control) of the Iraqi oil fields in 1972. When worldwide oil prices shot up in 1974, Iraq suddenly became wealthy and powerful. With money from oil sales, the government was at last able to begin developing the country. Hospitals and schools were built, and other modern development projects were planned. Iraq was on its way to becoming a modern industrialized nation.

President al-Bakr was assisted by his ambitious young cousin named Saddam Hussein. President al-Bakr allowed Saddam to take on more and more responsibility in the government. Saddam organized a secret intelligence service that would serve him well later as spies and informers. He established a militia similar to the National Guard in the United States that would counter the influence of the army. He installed his family members in key positions in the military and in government. As al-Bakr relinquished more and more control to Saddam, Saddam used the opportunity to assassinate his rivals and spread terror. As historian Geoff Simons describes,

> "Traitors" were shot, following [quick, fake] trials, after which the families of the victims would be presented with an official invoice to demand payment for the bullets that had killed their relatives. Such tactics were well designed to spread terror in the population and to further impress observers with Saddam's growing power.[14]

Finally, in 1979 al-Bakr retired from his position, and on July 16, 1979, Saddam Hussein declared himself president of Iraq and chairman of the Revolutionary Command Council. He quickly let people know what kind of government it would be by executing all those in the Baath Party who might oppose him. Saddam Hussein became the absolute ruler in Iraq.

WAR WITH IRAN

One of Saddam's first actions was to invade the neighboring country of Iran. In 1979 Iran was taken over by the popular Shiite religious leader, Ayatollah Khomeini. Iran became an Islamic state, whose government was founded on traditional laws and values found in the Koran. From Iran, Khomeini urged the Iraqi Shiite population to overthrow Saddam's government and establish an Islamic state there as well. A further conflict between Iran and Iraq was the centuries-old dispute over who controlled the Shatt al-Arab waterway.

Finally, war broke out between the two countries in September 1980. During the war, the main weapons supplier for Iraq was the United States. Fearing fundamentalist Islamic Iran and worried about disruption of the oil supply, the

SADDAM HUSSEIN— DICTATOR AND TYRANT

Saddam Hussein was born on April 28, 1937, in a mud hut in a small village near the town of Tikrit. Some accounts say that Saddam's father died before his birth. Others say that his father deserted the family. The name *Saddam* means "one who confronts and is bold." His mother remarried, and Saddam lived with his mother and stepfather, who was harsh and abusive. Saddam ran away when he was ten to live with his uncle in Tikrit. His uncle passed along to Saddam his hatred of foreigners, especially the British, as well as stories of the glorious Arab achievements in the time of the Arab caliphs. As a result, Saddam hated foreigners as an adult, and he dreamed of an Arab society that would revive the glorious days of Islam in its golden age.

When Saddam was eighteen, his uncle moved the family to Baghdad. At the time Baghdad was a place of unrest, with demonstrations and plots against the British-sponsored monarchy. Saddam joined the Baath Party when he was twenty and began to work his way up the party ranks. In 1959 Saddam took part in the attempted assassination of Abdul Karim Kassem. The attempt failed, but Saddam escaped to Syria, and then on to Cairo, Egypt. Kassem was killed in 1963 and Saddam returned to Iraq to work in the Baath Party organization. When the government of Arif turned on the Baath, Saddam was arrested and spent two years in jail before escaping. With General Ahmad Hasan al-Bakr, the Baath Party came to power in 1968. General al-Bakr surrounded himself with relatives from his home village of Tikrit, including Saddam Hussein. Under al-Bakr, Saddam began to build a base of power. When General al-Bakr retired, Saddam took power on July 16, 1979. Like all of the elite rulers in Iraq, Saddam was a Sunni Muslim, although the Baath government was secular.

United States felt it was in its best interests to help Saddam Hussein, even though government officials recognized he was a bloody dictator. The United States sold weapons, military equipment and other high technology, and military aircraft to Iraq, while it worked to prevent Iran from receiving arms. Much of the equipment was given to the Iraqis on credit. The United States also passed on information collected through aerial photographs of the region. Even though there was clear evidence that Iraq used chemical poison weapons against the Iranians, the United States continued to aid Iraq.

Despite the aid from the United States and other Western nations, the Iran-Iraq war dragged on until 1988, with neither side gaining a decisive victory. The war exhausted the Iraqi economy and people. It had cost Iraq about $450 billion and nearly 1 million lives, and it had crippled Iraq's oil production.

VIOLENCE AGAINST THE KURDS

Shortly after the war ended, Saddam turned his attention to the Kurds. During the war, the Kurds, always the enemy of Saddam and still hoping for independence, had joined Iranians in attacking Iraqi border towns. Saddam decided that he would destroy the Kurds once and for all. Male Kurds were arrested and shot. Their families were relocated, often being transported in trucks to camps in the desert and left to starve. Villages were then burned, and bulldozers buried what remained in the dirt, erasing all traces of their existence. In some cases, Iraq used chemical weapons on some Kurdish villages, immediately killing all the inhabitants. The use of these weapons (called weapons of mass destruction because they can destroy masses of people in a single attack) brought criticism from around the world.

Saddam's campaign against the Kurds resulted in the destruction of thousands of villages, and the death of about 50,000. Thousands of people—mainly women, children, and elderly people were relocated in terrible conditions. Saddam Hussein justified the action as necessary to force the people of the region to accept the authority of the state of Iraq. However, much of the world considered the attacks a brutal attempt at genocide—a deliberate attempt to destroy an entire ethnic group.

SADDAM'S WORLDVIEW

According to Saad al-Bazzaz, an Iraqi newspaper editor and TV producer who left Iraq in 1992, Saddam Hussein views the world from the perspective of a village patriarch, or headman. Saddam was born and raised in a village. In traditional village life, people are loyal to their own family, their tribe, and their village. They see outsiders as a threat. The family is ruled by the patriarch, and the village is ruled by the strongest of the patriarchs. Gaining and keeping power in whatever way possible is the most important political act, and loyalty to the village or tribe is the most important value. As Saad al-Bazzaz explains:

> [Saddam Hussein] is the ultimate Iraqi patriarch, the village leader who has seized a nation. Because he has come so far, he feels anointed by destiny. Everything he does is, by definition, the right thing to do. He has been chosen by Heaven to lead. Often in his life he has been saved by God, and each escape makes him more certain of his destiny. In recent years, in his speeches, he has begun using passages and phrases from the Koran, speaking the words as if they are his own. In the Koran, Allah says, "If you thank me, I will give you more." In the early nineties Saddam was on TV, presenting awards to military officers, and he said, "If you thank me, I will give you more." He no longer believes he is a normal person. . . . To him, strength is everything. To allow criticism or differences of opinion, to negotiate or compromise, to accede to the rule of law or to due process—these are signs of weakness.

THE PERSIAN GULF WAR

Iraq had not yet recovered from the war with Iran and the military campaign against the Kurds when Saddam Hussein began another military invasion. In 1990 Saddam Hussein invaded Kuwait, the neighboring country to the south, claiming it as part of Iraq. To Saddam, it was a step toward building a united Arab nation. Perhaps more importantly, he thought Kuwait's immense oil wealth could help Iraq recover from its economic losses during the Iran-Iraq war. After taking control of Kuwait, Iraq moved large numbers of troops to the border of Saudi Arabia. Western industrialized nations became alarmed at the prospect of an interruption in the flow of oil from the oilfields of Saudi Arabia and Kuwait.

The United States along with the United Nations organized a coalition, or alliance, of thirty-nine nations to pressure Iraq to withdraw from Kuwait. The leading members of the coalition included the United States, Egypt, France, Britain, Saudi Arabia, and Syria. The United States and its allies sent troops to defend Saudi territory. (This was the first time in modern history that non-Muslim troops had been stationed in Saudi Arabia, the site of many Islamic holy places sacred to Muslims. Many devout Muslims in Saudi Arabia and other Arab countries considered this a sacrilege and bitterly resented the presence of U.S. troops.)

As further pressure, the United Nations Security Council instituted trade sanctions against Iraq. This meant that Iraq could not export its oil, and goods from other nations could not enter Iraq. This embargo of export and import goods was meant to cripple the Iraqi economy and force Saddam Hussein to withdraw from Kuwait.

Despite the pressure, Iraq refused to withdraw from Kuwait. So, on January 16, 1991, the allies launched Operation Desert Storm. The war began with the allies bombing Iraq with sophisticated missiles. In February allied troops invaded Kuwait. They drove out the Iraqis and forced Iraq to agree to a cease-fire just 100 hours after ground troops landed. Despite Saddam's boast that he would be victorious in this "Mother of All Battles," the entire war lasted a mere 43 days. On the Iraq side, more than 100,000 soldiers were killed or wounded, and large numbers of civilians were killed and injured. The allied forces lost 149 killed and about 500 wounded.

Iraqi soldiers caused enormous damage in Kuwait. They damaged oil wells, causing millions of gallons of oil to spill into Persian Gulf waters, which killed thousands of seabirds and huge numbers of fish. They set fire to other wells, which caused smoke so thick and black that the sunlight was blocked out.

A damaged oil well burns out of control in Kuwait. Iraqi soldiers destroyed many oil wells during the Persian Gulf War.

AFTERMATH OF THE WAR

The Persian Gulf War was over, but Saddam Hussein was still in power. Allied troops did not pursue the retreating Iraqi army into Baghdad. Allied leaders had accomplished their goal of forcing Iraq to withdraw from Kuwait. Not wishing to risk more losses to their military forces, they decided to avoid any further interference in Iraq. The allies believed that Saddam's forces had been so thoroughly defeated and humiliated that Saddam's own people would remove him.

At first it seemed they would be right about Saddam's fate. The Kurds revolted in the north. In the south, Shiite Muslims turned against the Sunni government. They captured the cities of Basra, Najaf, and Karbala. Although a major portion of the Iraqi army had been destroyed, Saddam still had his elite troops, the Republican Guard. He sent these troops against the Shiites, who were defeated and driven into the marshes, where they were hunted down and killed. He then turned on the Kurds. Without outside support, the Kurds were quickly defeated, and some 2 million fled across the border into Turkey for refuge.

Iraq had not allowed foreign humanitarian aid agencies to bring food and medical supplies to the Kurds or Shiites, who were suffering from lack of these necessities. Seeing the plight of the Kurds in the north and the Shiites in the south, the United Nations ordered Iraq to allow humanitarian aid agencies to assist the people. "No-fly" zones were marked off in the north and in the south over the Kurdish and Shiite areas. Iraqi planes were not permitted to fly over those zones, and Iraqi army troops were not permitted to enter the zones. U.S. warplanes patrolled the area to enforce the no-fly rule and protect the people in those areas. In the safe haven under the protection of the no-fly zone, the Kurds set up a semiautonomous region, with local officials taking responsibility for the welfare of the people.

Meanwhile, nations of the world feared that Iraq was continuing to develop chemical and biological weapons and was attempting to develop nuclear weapons. In 1991, the United Nations Security Council set up UNSCOM (UN Special Commission) to locate and destroy Iraq's weapons of mass destruction. Under the terms of the peace treaty, Iraq was to allow weapons inspectors to make sure that all of the weapons were destroyed. Once the inspectors had completed

Members of UNSCOM leave Iraq in 1998.

their task, the sanctions imposed against Iraq would be lifted, allowing Iraq to sell its oil on the world market and import goods from other countries.

However, the sanctions have never been fully removed because Saddam Hussein has never fully cooperated with the weapons inspectors. At various times, they were denied access to certain areas or refused permission to inspect anything at all. Finally, in 1998, convinced that Saddam Hussein would not willingly cooperate with inspections, the inspectors left altogether. Then, hoping to force Saddam Hussein's compliance with UNSCOM, U.S. and British forces once again resumed bombing military targets in Iraq. Despite the damage and casualties caused by the bombing, the Iraqis refused to allow the inspectors to return and complete their work.

Although the sanctions were meant to put pressure on Saddam, the world soon realized that it was the ordinary people—not Saddam Hussein—who suffered most from the embargo. To ease their suffering, in 1996 the United Nations agreed to allow Iraq to sell a limited amount of oil to buy necessary food and medicines for its people. This "oil-for-food" program has done little to help average Iraqis, however, because most of the benefits of the oil sales never reach them. According to U.S. government sources, medicine imported through the "oil for food" program is sold by the government to private hospitals at outrageous prices. Saddam continues to build monuments and elaborate palaces to himself and to enrich his top officials, while many Iraqi citizens still suffer from hunger or malnutrition and lack of medical care. The children especially have suffered; thousands have died every year from malnutrition and preventable diseases.

In the late 1970s and early 1980s, Iraq's plentiful oil resources seemed to promise prosperity for its people. The country was building a strong, well-educated, and prosperous middle class. All Iraqi children were provided with an education. Iraq's health care system was the best in the Middle East. But two decades of war and sanctions have seriously damaged Iraq's economy, dramatically affecting the Iraqi way of life.

THE IRAQI WAY OF LIFE

In normal times, life in Iraq is a rich combination of ancient traditions and modern practices. Many citizens—especially those in rural areas—still follow the old ways in their choice of dress, housing, and family structure. Others choose a modern way of life, much like those in Western nations, or a combination of traditional and modern practices. However, the Persian Gulf War and the consequent UN sanctions have had a dramatic impact on the Iraqi way of life.

CITY LIFE AND RURAL LIFE

Until the 1980s, the Iraqi people enjoyed an increasingly prosperous life, with a growing economy and a growing middle class. Today, however, every aspect of Iraqi life has been affected by the consequences of the Persian Gulf War and the UN sanctions. But in normal times, life in a modern Iraqi city is similar to life in Western cities.

The wealthy who live in the city are likely to work in business or government. Middle-class people are often office workers, craftspeople, or small business owners. Poorer city residents work as laborers. Many people from rural areas commute to the city from nearby villages to work as laborers and in factories.

Many city dwellers prefer to wear Western clothing. The men dress in suits or shirts and slacks. Women wear dresses or skirts and blouses. Most Iraqi women observe Islamic standards of modesty and do not wear sleeveless dresses or short skirts. However, city women often wear make-up and jewelry, and some like to dye their hair. City laborers and people from rural areas usually prefer to wear the long, flowing robes traditional for Arabs.

In rural areas, people generally farm. Most farmers grow vegetables. The government owns much of Iraqi farmland, and most farmers lease the land from the government.

Farmers pitch hay in the heat of day. Many citizens of rural Iraq cling to farming as a way of life.

However, the life of a farmer is challenging, and Iraq still relies heavily on imported food. Much of the land is too arid for farming, although the government is developing new irrigation systems. The major crops grown include wheat, barley, grapes, rice, tomatoes, and dates. Most meat, poultry, and dairy products, as well as sugar, must be imported. Much of the imported foods are in short supply or out of reach of most Iraqis today. A few rural people are herders. In the north, Kurds raise livestock such as goats and sheep. In the west, Bedouin nomads generally keep goats, sheep, and camels.

Much of Iraqi agriculture has been seriously damaged since the Persian Gulf War and the economic sanctions imposed by the United Nations. Irrigation systems were damaged in the bombings, and the sanctions have prevented Iraq from acquiring the necessary materials to repair the damage. Consequently, agricultural production has been affected.

HOMES

While much of Iraq's housing, in rural areas as well as in cities, has been damaged by war, people still usually prefer traditional Iraqi housing. Although middle-class city people frequently live in apartment buildings, wealthy city dwellers usually live in pleasant suburbs around the city. Traditional Iraqi houses in urban areas are made of brick or mud. They are usually large, with two stories and a central open courtyard. Houses often have balconies or bay windows that overlook the narrow streets. The first floor usually has two large reception or sitting rooms, one for men and one for women. This style house is ancient, dating back to 2500 B.C.

The roof of the traditional home is used as a living space as well. Even though most of Iraq has extremely hot summers, very few houses have air conditioning. The family sleeps on the roof at night during the hot months. They often have a television on the roof which the family gathers around during the evening. The roof has a terrace with a low wall or parapet for privacy.

In rural villages, homes are constructed of mud brick, with a roof made of reeds or twigs. The most common type of home is a low, rectangular, one-room hut with no windows. A walled courtyard in the rear is used to keep animals.

In the marshes, Madan villages are built in shallow water in the center of stands of reeds. Individual homes are built on

THE TRADITIONAL COFFEE HOUSE

A central part of the traditional Iraqi way of life was the coffee house. The coffee house was an important community gathering place for men only, a hub where news was exchanged, business deals were negotiated, politics were discussed. Travelers came to the coffee house, bringing news from other places, and learning the local news. High school boys met to study for exams; possibilities for potential arranged marriages were discussed. Sometimes special social events took place at the coffee house, accompanied by music. Men sat on wooden benches around the tables, drinking thick sweet coffee served in small teacups and highly sweetened tea served in small glasses. During much of the year, the men sat on benches outside, drinking tea or coffee, playing backgammon, or just talking.

platforms made of stacked layers of reeds and mud. From a distance, villages appear to be on islands in the water. Homes are arched huts made of reeds surrounded by low reed fences. However, the marshes are being deliberately drained by the Iraqi government, and few Madan villages remain.

FAMILIES

One of the important elements in the Iraqi way of life is family. The structure of Iraqi families usually follows traditional patterns. Nearly all Iraqis are Muslims, and Islamic law and values guide social relations. Therefore, most groups in society—Kurds or Arabs, urban or rural—follow the same or similar traditions in family affairs. Traditional families usually consist of an extended family, usually three generations, that occupies one house or two adjacent houses. The family consists of grandparents, their sons and sons' wives, and their sons' children. Sometimes other dependent relatives are included, such as the unmarried sister of the oldest male. In recent years, with the influence of Western practices, the nuclear family—a man, wife, and children—is becoming fairly common in large cities.

The practice of polygamy—having two or more wives—is allowed by the Islamic religion, and in the past it was not uncommon for the extended family to include two or more

 INDOCTRINATING THE YOUTH
Like other absolute dictators of the past century, Saddam Hussein believes in indoctrinating citizens at a young age. In *Iraq: From Sumer to Saddam*, author Geoff Simons quotes Saddam Hussein describing his beliefs about teaching young people:

> The Party and the State should be their family, their father and mother. . . . You must encircle the adults through their sons. . . . Teach students and pupils to contradict their parents. . . . You must place in every corner a son of the revolution, with a trustworthy eye and a firm mind who receives his instruction from the responsible centre of the revolution.

For Saddam Hussein, keeping the citizens obedient to him and keeping himself in power begin with shaping the minds of the young.

wives of one man, along with the women's children. The practice is declining, especially among modern urban Iraqis, but it is still occasionally found in both the extended family and the nuclear family.

The head of the household is the oldest male. In theory, he has absolute authority over all members of his household. He manages the economic affairs of the family, decides on his children's education, and makes the final decision in all matters. Respect for his authority is carefully taught to children, and, in rural families, even adult, married sons are expected to obey their fathers.

Traditionally, large families are highly valued in Iraqi society. A large number of children, especially sons, is regarded as a source of pride for the father. Among the poorer families, children are also considered an economic asset. Children can work and contribute to the family at an early age. The birth of a child, especially a boy, is cause for celebration.

RELATIONS BETWEEN MEN AND WOMEN

Men and women in Iraq—as in other Muslim countries—rarely socialize with each other. Arranged marriages are still the tradition, and marriage between cousins is common and often preferred, because it keeps the girl, as well as any inheritance she may have, within her family.

Arranging a marriage is a family matter. Generally, the negotiations are carried on between the parents of the bride and groom. The part played by the mother in the negotiations varies from group to group. Among the Marsh Arabs, fathers conduct all the negotiations, and the mothers have no say in the final choice. Among the Kurds, mothers choose prospective partners for their sons or daughters, but the fathers of the two families involved make the final arrangements between themselves. Part of the arrangements in Iraqi marriages include a "bride price" paid by the man or his family to the woman's father. Among educated city dwellers, the practice of arranged marriages is changing. More and more, young people choose their own marriage partners. Usually, however, parents must still approve the choice.

Traditional marriage ceremonies involve two parts. At the engagement, the couple's parents invite friends and family to the bride's house to make the announcement. The actual signing of the marriage contract takes place later and consists of a gathering of friends and relatives, along with a judge from a religious court who presides over the signing of the contract. A typical village wedding among the Kurds includes a breakfast feast followed by a day of dancing and celebrating. Men and women each celebrate separately. In the cities, weddings generally involve a noisy parade through the streets followed by a grand feast. Women marry quite young, at fifteen or sixteen, while the men tend to marry older—usually in their mid to late twenties.

WOMEN'S STATUS

The traditional role of women has gradually changed in Iraq over the past few decades, but despite some advances by women, men are still dominant in Iraqi society. Educated, middle-class women who live in the cities are more likely to have more freedom of choice in areas such as choosing a marriage partner, deciding whether to wear traditional or Western clothing, and having a job outside the home. In the 1980s, nearly half of all Iraqi teachers were women. Almost a third of the Iraqi physicians were women. Women could become accountants, pharmacists, dentists, factory workers, and civil servants. Most of these women workers were city dwellers.

On the surface, Iraq is a country that allows women a measure of freedom. When the Baath Party originally came to power, the General Federation of Iraqi Women was founded as an extension of the party, courting women by offering a chance at equal rights. Officially, women share all the rights of men. They can vote and hold elected office. They are guaranteed these rights by the country's constitution, which states that all Iraqis are equal under the law.

In reality, however, women are not always treated as equals. In 1988, a law legalizing "honor killings" was passed. This law permitted men to kill their wives if they had been judged guilty of adultery, a crime for which it is difficult to prove innocence. Honor killings are widely condemned as a violation of human rights. Though the law was repealed a couple of years later, many Iraqi officials continue to ignore the practice of honor killings.

Since the Persian Gulf War, life under UN sanctions has made it increasingly difficult for women to maintain their independence. The economy has suffered severely under the

Two young women walk through an Iraqi marketplace. Women enjoy a measure of freedom under the Iraqi constitution.

sanctions, and there is an extremely high rate of unemployment. Many women have lost their jobs. Without work, Iraqi women are unable to support themselves and must rely on men. With the loss of economic independence, they have lost their best means to self-determination, and their situation continues to deteriorate.

EDUCATION

An important factor in improving the lives of women and of all Iraqis is education. Education has been a high priority of Iraq since its establishment as a nation. In the nineteenth century the literacy rate—the percentage of the population that can read and write—was only about 1 percent. Today, nearly 60 percent of the people can read and write.

The government's intense program to educate its citizens has been one of its more successful efforts. In addition to educating young people, the government has provided instruction in reading and writing for people between fifteen and forty-five who are illiterate.

Schooling begins at age six for all Iraqi children, who are required by law to attend until they are twelve years old. Nearly every village has at least a primary school. Secondary schools are provided for children beyond age twelve.

The curriculum in the primary schools focuses on religion, Arabic language and penmanship, arithmetic, geography, and history. Upper grades of secondary schools prepare students for admission to college. Students of secondary schools choose between a science or a literary curriculum, depending on their interests. In addition to the specialized section curriculum, the curriculum in both sections includes religion, Arabic, English, and history, as well as child care and home-making for girls.

Iraqi schoolchildren sit in neat rows under the watchful eye of their teacher. Boys and girls must attend school until age twelve.

TERROR IN DAILY LIFE

Saddam Hussein's greatest weapon, and his people's greatest fear, is the organized system of terror that he uses to control the people. Any criticism of Saddam, or the party, however slight, can bring arrest, imprisonment, torture, and even execution. People are never sure who is a spy and who will report even the most innocent comment.

He maintains his system of terror by surrounding himself with people whose loyalty is assured. Most of his closest advisers and people in key positions in government are relatives and people from his native village of Tikrit. He bribes his supporters with high salaries, expensive homes and cars, and other rewards. He handpicks the people who run his well-organized State Internal Security service, whose purpose is to spy on citizens, and the Baath Party Security office, which spies on Baath Party members, making sure that they remain loyal to Saddam.

In *Iraq: From Sumer to Saddam,* author Geoff Simons reports that "Iraq . . . has become a nation of informers. Party members are said to be required to inform on family, friends, and acquaintances, including other Party members. . . . Teachers reportedly ask pupils about their parents' views." Failure to inform can bring severe punishment. Simons describes the case of a man who did not report someone who made jokes about Saddam Hussein. The man who failed to report the incident was arrested, along with his three sons and a son-in-law. They were tortured and executed, and the family home was destroyed.

This severe brutality spreads terror throughout the population and effectively achieves Saddam's purpose: to control the people.

Vocational education is also offered to students not interested in higher education at the universities. Some vocational training courses include industrial training such as mechanical and electrical work, and agricultural training, including farm management, soil chemistry, and methods of irrigation.

Universities are located in the cities of Baghdad, Basra, Erbil, Mosul, and Tikrit, and there are a variety of colleges and institutes for agriculture, business, and technology. Some academic courses of study include dentistry, economics, education, engineering, medicine, pharmacology, industrial engineering, and natural sciences.

Today, the enrollment in school has seriously declined. Many children must work at odd jobs to help their families survive, because the economic sanctions have caused severe shortages and loss of jobs.

LIVING WITH ECONOMIC SANCTIONS

The central fact that affects nearly every aspect of Iraqi life is the embargo imposed by economic sanctions. The United Nations first placed sanctions against Iraq that called for embargo of goods going out of and coming into Iraq when Iraq invaded Kuwait in 1990. The sanctions were intended as an alternative to war and meant to persuade Saddam Hussein to withdraw his troops from Kuwait. The nations of the world reasoned that a rational leader would not stand by and watch the economy of his country be destroyed and his people suffer severe hardships. However, Saddam refused to withdraw his troops, war followed, and UN sanctions remained in place.

Because Iraq depends upon many imported foods, which are now blocked by the sanctions, hunger and malnutrition are common. In 1996 the United Nations agreed to allow Iraq to sell a limited amount of oil to buy necessary food and medicines for the people. However, except in the relatively autonomous region of Iraqi Kurdistan, where the Kurds are free from interference by the government in Baghdad, the "oil-for-food" program has offered only limited relief for the average Iraqi. The government diverts much of the food and medicines for its own uses.

Even though food and consumer goods are imported illegally from neighboring nations, only well-off Iraqis—those who are part of Saddam Hussein's elite or who are loyal government employees—can afford to buy them. The majority of Iraqis, including those who were once professionals such as engineers and doctors, are poorly paid, if they have work at all, and suffer severe hardships. Many unemployed try to survive by selling odds and ends—old magazines, used wiring, old furniture. As one reporter who visited Iraq describes,

> One man, displaying a dozen pairs of plastic sandals, breaks into a smile as he talks of his days at the university, studying computer science. When the UN embargo was imposed, he dropped out to help his parents and

five siblings, putting off plans to get married. They sold their house and moved into [rented] lodgings, then [sold their] books and ornaments, then [sold their] furniture. They have a few cooking pots still, and a change of clothes.[15]

Even the air Iraqis breathe is affected by the embargo. Air pollution has become a serious problem. Automobiles cannot be repaired because of the lack of parts, which cannot be imported because of the embargo. Broken-down cars with broken-down engines and exhaust systems create serious air pollution.

The lack of clean water and living with raw sewage can be deadly for many Iraqis. Bombs dropped on Baghdad and elsewhere have cracked the underground water lines. These cracks allow the groundwater to seep into the water system,

A mother tends to her malnourished son. UN sanctions have reduced supplies of food and medicine.

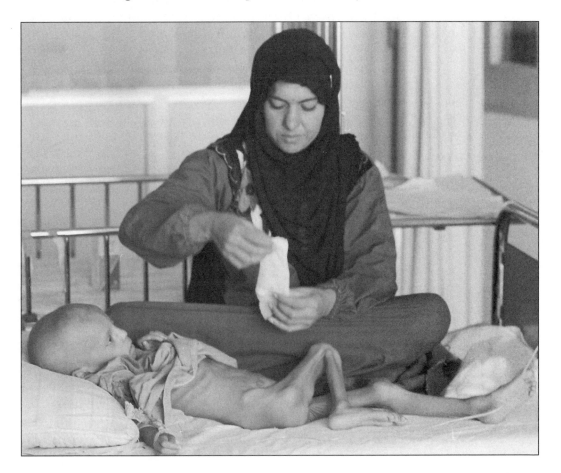

contaminating the fresh water. In many places, tap water is cloudy and tastes putrid. Pregnant women do not dare drink it, for fear that the pollutants will harm their unborn child. In the countryside, half the population has no running water at all.

Electric power generation is down by 50 percent, so some parts of the country regularly suffer electricity blackouts for nine to eighteen hours. Power plants cannot be repaired because the parts needed are limited by the embargo. According to a report by the Middle East Research and Information Project, "Electrical shortages, worst during the hot summers, spoil food and medicine and stop water purification, sewage treatment and irrigated agriculture, interfering with all aspects of life." [16]

Living with sanctions is hardest in the area of health care, and children are the most vulnerable. The unsanitary water causes serious diseases such as dysentery, which can be deadly to young children. Serious air pollution has caused a dramatic increase in respiratory illnesses among children and adults. Lack of adequate food has caused malnutrition in children, which in turn makes them more susceptible to disease. Lack of antibiotics and other medical supplies prevents doctors from curing them.

According to Kathy Kelly, founder of Voices in the Wilderness, an organization that attempts to help suffering Iraqi people, "Iraq used to be a sophisticated society where the greatest childhood medical problem was obesity." [17] It has been estimated that now as many as 5,000 to 6,000 Iraqi children die every month from preventable or curable diseases. The infant mortality rate is sixty deaths for every 1,000 live births. (In the United States, the infant mortality is seven deaths for every 1,000 live births.) According to a study of childhood mortality done by the United Nations Children's Fund (UNICEF), 131 children under five years old die for every 1,000 born.

In January 2001 two Canadian doctors visited an Iraqi pediatric hospital. Dr. Eric Hoskins offers this description, of just one of many children he saw suffering:

> Four-year-old Mohamed arrived at the hospital more than a month ago with a fever. His mother, unable to afford the approximately 10-cent daily fee, took him home after only a few days. Mohamed then had a massive seizure, lost consciousness and was brought back to

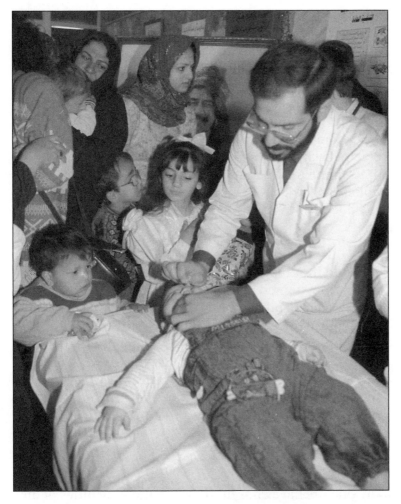

A child is immunized against polio in a crowded hospital room. Shortages of space and medical supplies threaten the health of the Iraqi people.

hospital. There was no oxygen in the hospital, so he suffered irreversible brain damage. Dr. Ali [the hospital chief of staff] pays for his medicines and hospital fees. [18]

The shortage of medicines and hospital supplies has devastating effects. According to Dr. Hoskins, the problems abound:

A shortage of medicines, no painkillers, few antibiotics, no feeding tubes, disposable syringes being used over and over again, no antiseptics to cleanse wounds, doctors and nurses performing truly heroic deeds. In Canada, I could have saved these children. Here, I was helpless. [19]

Pharmacy shelves are nearly empty, and what remain are drugs that have expired or are near the expiration date. Imported medicines are smuggled into Iraq, but only the rich can afford them. The poor resort to "home remedies." Even prescription pads are in short supply because of the shortage of paper, and doctors write prescriptions on scraps of paper.

Lack of medicines and medical supplies are not the only problem. Lack of up-to-date medical training is becoming a serious problem. Without livable salaries, sufficient medical supplies, and adequate medical training and information, many doctors live with discouragement, as Dr. Hoskins describes:

> Dr. Ali Hammid, the hospital chief of staff, is a 29-year-old internist who lives at the hospital. He sleeps on a urine-stained mat on the floor of the "Resident's Room." Due to inflation [of currency], his salary is now the equivalent of $2 a day, most of which he spends buying supplies for patients who cannot afford them. "I am doing this for humanity," he explains. "I have so much sadness and anxiety. I never see my wife or my family. All of my medical books are more than 10 years old. I do not know whether our treatment is right anymore." [20]

DESPERATE MEASURES

Many doctors have chosen to escape the difficulties of life in Iraq and have left to work in other countries. The ones who stay, or who cannot leave, resort to ingenious and desperate methods to help in their practice. According to an article in the medical journal *Lancet*, a senior surgeon "has learned the skills of preparing liquid soap out of chemicals in order to be able to scrub properly for [surgery]." The journal goes on to explain that "A urology textbook was taken into the country as a gift. Within days the recipient had made bound copies to sell to his surgical colleagues, thus helping to alleviate both his own poverty and his colleagues' lack of information." [21]

Even though the wars of the 1980s and 1990s have disrupted the Iraqi way of life in many ways, Iraqi tradition remains strong. Family ties remain the center of Iraqi life, despite the damage done to the economy and the education system. People still send their children to school where possible, and families work together to care for one another. The traditions of Iraqi life help hold society together, even in the face of devastating economic problems. And part of the tradition is nurturing a rich cultural life.

6

CULTURE IN IRAQ

From ancient times, religion, art, architecture, and poetry have been central to the lives of people in the region. Today, despite the hardships faced by modern Iraqis, they carry on many of the cultural practices of their ancestors.

RELIGION

Since the seventh century A.D., Islam has been the dominant religion in what is now Iraq. About 97 percent of Iraqis are Muslims. Over 60 percent of Iraqi Muslims are Shiite. Although the Sunnis are in the minority, most of the members of the ruling Baath Party are Sunnis. Many Shiites resent the monopoly on government power held by the Sunnis. About 3 percent of the people are Christian, who mainly live in the north.

Modern Iraq is a secular state—that is, its government is not based on laws found in the Koran. Other religions are tolerated. Nevertheless, Islam remains a very important part of the lives of the people and of the nation.

The word *Islam* means "surrender" or "submission." Muslims strive to submit to the will of God (or Allah in Arabic). The central belief in Islam is that there is only one God and Muhammad is his prophet. The Koran, the holy book of Islam, contains the teachings of God as given to Muhammad. The record of Muhammad's acts and sayings is recorded in the Hadith. The Koran and the Hadith form the sacred teachings of Islam.

The religious life of Muslims is governed by the Five Pillars of Islam. The first is reciting the *shahada* (which means "bear witness"), which says, "There is no God but God, and Muhammad is his prophet." To become a Muslim, one must recite the shahada.

Praying five times a day is the second pillar. Praying is the most important part of the Muslim's religious practice. Muslims pray five times a day—at dawn, at noontime, in the middle of the afternoon, at sunset, and at night. Because the time of prayer is determined by the sun, not by a clock, prayer times are announced by a *muezzin,* a person who calls people to prayer from a minaret. A minaret is a tower next to a mosque. Friday is the special day of prayer for Muslims. All over Iraq, people gather at mosques to pray and hear short sermons by religious leaders called *imams.*

Fasting from sunrise to sunset during the month of Ramadan is another pillar of Islam. The months of the Islamic calendar are based on the phases of the moon, which means that Ramadan falls at different seasons. According to Islamic beliefs, Ramadan is the month in which the first part of the Koran was revealed to Muhammad. From sunrise to sunset during the entire month of Ramadan, Muslims cannot take any food, drink (including water), or tobacco, or engage in

Men gesture while praying at a mosque. Daily prayer is the second pillar of Islam, the dominant religion in Iraq.

sexual intercourse. According to the Koran, eating and drinking are permissible at any time during the night, "until you can plainly distinguish a white thread from a black thread by the daylight: then keep the fast until night." [22] The purpose of the fast is to help people practice self-restraint and spiritual contemplation. Fasting is very demanding, especially when Ramadan falls during the heat of the summer season. The sick or injured, the elderly, and pregnant women are excused from fasting.

Almsgiving, or giving to the poor, is the fourth pillar of Islam. Devout Muslims practice almsgiving throughout the

 ## MUHAMMAD AND THE ANGEL GABRIEL

To Muslims, Muhammad is the last prophet of Allah, or God. According to Islamic tradition as recorded in the Koran, Muhammad became the prophet when the Angel Gabriel descended from heaven and revealed Allah's nature to him.

Muhammad was born about A.D. 570 in the city of Mecca, in what is now Saudi Arabia. Muhammad was orphaned as a child, and he was raised by his grandfather and later by his uncle. He worked as a trader with them, visiting many areas throughout the Arab world.

Muhammad married Khadija, a wealthy widow more than ten years older than he. One day, while meditating, Muhammad had a vision. According to Muslim belief, Muhammad's vision was of the angel Gabriel, who told Muhammad that he was to become a prophet and preach God's message. Muhammad continued to have visions and soon began to preach publicly.

According to Muhammad, the Koran is the record of words spoken by Gabriel, memorized by the prophet, and recited to his companions, who wrote them down. Muhammad even memorized and had recorded the words Gabriel used when greeting the prophet:

> Recite thou, in the name of thy Lord who created; created man from clots of blood: Recite thou! For thy Lord is the most beneficent, who hath taught the use of the pen; hath taught man that which he knoweth not. (Koran, sura xcvi)

Muhammad received many revelations after this, though not after some tribulations on his part.

year, but especially during the celebration that follows the end of Ramadan.

Making a pilgrimage to the city of Mecca in Saudi Arabia is the fifth pillar for all Muslims, including Iraqi Muslims. All Muslims who are physically and financially able are required by the Koran to make a pilgrimage, called the *hajj,* to Mecca at least once during their life. Once the pilgrim arrives at Mecca, the rites take several days and are performed at the beginning of the twelfth month of the Islamic calendar. The rites center around the Kaaba, an empty building in the Great Mosque in the city of Mecca. Muslims consider the Kaaba to be the very first house of worship built by the Old Testament figure Abraham and his son Ishmael. The pilgrims must wear certain garments and walk around the Kaaba seven times in a counterclockwise direction.

Devout Muslims circle the Kaaba in the Great Mosque in the sacred city of Mecca.

THE SHIITES

Though Islam is a single religion and all Muslims share the same basic beliefs, there are two major branches of Islam, which are at odds with each other. Sunni Islam is practiced by about 90 percent of the world's Muslims and can be found from the North African coast to Indonesia. Only about 10 percent of Muslims belong to the other branch, Shia Islam, and Shiites, as they are known, live primarily in Iran and Iraq.

The original split between the two branches stems from a dispute regarding who would be the leader of the Muslims after the death of the prophet Muhammad. The Shiites believe that Ali, a son-in-law of Muhammad, was the rightful fourth caliph (leader) of the Muslims. Ali was never fully accepted by all Muslims, many of whom disliked the fact that Ali had become caliph with the aid of the murderers of the third caliph, Uthman. Ali was killed at the Battle of Karbala, near Kufah in Iraq, but his son continued his dynasty. The Shiites follow the leaders that are descended from Ali, and Shiite means "Party of Ali."

Because most Iraqis are Muslim, religion plays an important part in the life of the nation. Another important element of Iraqi culture is the arts.

ANCIENT ARTS

Few countries have such an ancient and rich tradition of art and architecture as Iraq, since few countries have hosted such an impressive succession of civilizations. The Iraq Museum contains archaeological treasures from the Sumerians up through the Abbasids. Artifacts include jewelry, pottery, clay figures, carved stone, and textiles. The remains of ancient buildings still stand, and archaeological excavations have revealed many other ancient buildings, including ziggurats, temples, and palaces.

The artifacts are not only impressive works of art themselves; they also give clues to life in ancient times. One of the richest works is a 4,500-year-old wooden panel called the Standard of Ur, found during an excavation of the city of Ur. Inlaid with shells and blue stone called lapis lazuli, the panel shows figures from all social classes: soldiers in battle, the king holding a banquet, commoners with their livestock and produce. Archaeologists can learn a lot about ancient civilizations from the artifacts they leave behind.

One of the most impressive pieces of ancient architecture is the main gate of the city of Babylon, which was built by Nebuchadnezzar. The gate was built of bricks that had been baked in a kiln and cemented together with tar. Originally, the gate had an outer layer of enameled bricks that were decorated with brilliantly colored enamel images of bulls and dragons. The structure is now kept in a museum.

VISUAL ARTS
Modern visual art includes heavy emphasis on tradition. Traditional Islam forbids the representation of human beings in art in religious settings, because the Koran forbids idols or

Built by the Babylonian king Nebuchadnezzar around 575 B.C., the Ishtar Gate remains one of Iraq's most impressive pieces of architecture.

anything that may be seen as idolatry (the worship of anything, usually an object, other than Allah). In traditional Islam, most representations of humans or animals are considered idols. However, there are some human figures in Islamic art. This kind of art is limited to secular and usually private spheres. Most of the Islamic art that is publicly available is called "decorative art."

Under the Arab caliphs, Islamic artists used elaborate and beautiful geometric patterns in mosaic tile to decorate mosques and other buildings. Much of that is preserved in the old mosques around Iraq.

There are three main forms used in decorative art: calligraphy, geometry, and floral patterns. Modern Iraqi artists still practice the art of calligraphy—the elaborate and ornate Arabic lettering. Calligraphy is often used in copying parts of the Koran or to decorate walls of mosques. In Islamic art, calligraphy is always in Arabic and is often a verse from the Koran. For this reason, calligraphy is prominently featured on religious buildings, like mosques. Calligraphic texts are often used to frame other objects, such as doors and windows, and may form a border for other forms of art.

Geometry is used often in Islamic art. Many Iraqi artists create highly complex geometric patterns, often making use of overlapping pieces to create three-dimensional effects. In these designs, symmetry is an essential trait. Floral patterns are an extension of the geometric. Some of these patterns are called "arabesque," a style of art that uses curving patterns of flowers and vines.

In addition, Iraq celebrates modern sculpture and painting. The painter Abd al Kadir ar Rassah (1872–1951) is considered the "father of modern art" in Iraq. Works by modern artists are exhibited today in galleries and museums, especially in Baghdad. The style of contemporary Iraqi art ranges from the realistic to impressionist and abstract. Many modern Iraqi artists use bright, vibrant colors. Some of the themes include desert landscapes, often featuring the fabled Arabian horses or Bedouin and their camels, as well as scenes from traditional Iraqi life, such as people at prayer or an outdoor bazaar.

MUSIC

Tradition also plays a part in music. Iraqi folk music is played at events such as weddings and other special occasions. Instruments include stringed instruments such as a type of zither, an instrument that resembles a lute, and instruments that are similar to fiddles. Iraqis sometimes use drums called *dumbuks.*

Iraq also has many popular contemporary musicians. Both male and female vocalists record their music on CDs, but despite the modern technology, contemporary Iraqi music often features traditional instruments and a style that is favored by most Iraqis.

The Baghdad School of Music and Ballet was established in 1970 for students of music and dance. Iraq also has a National Symphony Orchestra. Although Western classical music is not as popular in Iraq as other forms of music, the symphony orchestra is composed of musicians who were born and raised in Iraq, and the performances are well attended.

LITERATURE

Perhaps the art most loved by Iraqis is literature. Iraq has an ancient literary tradition that goes back to ancient Mesopotamia. The most famous early epic poem is the Sumerian story of Gilgamesh, a warrior king, and his search for eternal life.

However, the Koran (also spelled Qur'an), which is the holy book of Islam, occupies a central place in Arab literature. The Koran consists of 114 chapters, which range in length from a few lines to over 200 lines. Much of the language in the Koran is rich and powerful rhymed Arabic prose, which Muslims believe cannot be matched by human beings, a sign that it is the language of God revealed to Muhammad. Verses from the Koran are recited in Arabic by Iraqi Muslims—and Muslims all over the world—every day during their daily prayers.

Arabs have a long history of poetry and storytelling. Poetry is by far the most popular form of literature in Iraq. Iraqis, like Arabs throughout the Middle East, enjoy listening to and reciting poetry, and many write poetry as well. The strongly rhythmical traditional Arab music is associated with a love of poetry. Following ancient custom, poetry is composed to be read aloud. In Iraq, poetry is a common form of expression. One does not have to be a professional poet to write poetry, and average people frequently compose poems in honor of special events or people. Poetry readings are well attended.

RECREATION

The most important form of recreation for Iraqis is sports. Iraqis love sports of all kinds. They follow horse racing, basketball, weight lifting, boxing, and volleyball. They also play board games such as chess and backgammon in their homes.

But by far, the most popular sport in Iraq is soccer—or football as it is called in Iraq and most other nations of the world. Iraqi boys play soccer in the streets, on vacant lots, in cities and villages throughout the country. Iraqis follow not only their own soccer teams but also the popular European teams as well. National league games are broadcast regularly on television, and fans crowd the stadiums to watch the games live.

People in all walks of life are fans. According to Iraqi soccer coach Adnan Hammed, Saddam Hussein himself "is a big fan of sports and soccer. There are plans to build stadiums all over, not only for soccer, but other sports as well." [23] Saddam Hussein's son, Uday Hussein, is the head of the Iraq Football Federation.

Iraqi soccer teams tour other countries. The great hope for the national team is to compete in the World Cup, the world championship of soccer held every four years. According to the team's coach, "That would make a great impression on the younger generation and bring great joy to our people." [24]

MOVIES, NEWSPAPERS, TELEVISION, RADIO

Until the advent of Saddam Hussein, films were another popular form of entertainment, although they were subject to government censorship. Today, Iraqi filmmakers in exile produce feature-length films, often dealing with life in Iraq during wartime and with the suffering of the people under Saddam Hussein. However, such films criticizing Iraq never appear in Iraqi theaters, where the government strictly censors all films. The government does produce documentary films, often dealing with the glories of the Iraqi past.

The government also controls all of the media in Iraq. Privately owned newspapers were banned in 1967, but by the late 1980s the government was producing seven daily newspapers. All news agencies and print and broadcast media are owned by the government and the Baath Party. The media do not report news or opinions that are critical of the government.

The government also operates two television channels, which air selected shows, some from other Arab countries. In addition to programming such as Egyptian comedy shows, songs and poems written by citizens in praise of Saddam Hussein are aired daily.

Players compete in a soccer match in Baghdad. Soccer, or football as it is called in Iraq, is the most popular sport in the country.

The Republic of Iraq Radio is the official state radio broadcasting service. Voice of Youth radio is owned by Uday Hussein, Saddam Hussein's son. A few Kurdish radio stations operate from northern Iraq, outside the zone of influence of the government in Baghdad. Some radio services such as Radio Free Iraq, backed by the United States, are operated outside Iraq but aimed at the Iraqi people to inform them of events in the outside world and to counteract Iraqi government propaganda.

The government strictly controls all domestic programming. Broadcasters can receive the death penalty for airing programs that insult Saddam Hussein or other government officials.

TREE OF LIFE

People in ancient Mesopotamia began growing date palms and harvesting dates 5,000 years ago. Today, dates are Iraq's most important agricultural product and a staple of the Iraqi diet. Large date palm plantations are located in the south near the confluence of the Tigris and Euphrates rivers. In the Muslim tradition, the date palm is called the "Tree of Life." Many Iraqis have date palm trees in their gardens. Date palms supply more than just fruit. Palm leaves are used for matting and for making paper. Rope is made from bark fibers. The wood is used in building. A syrup is made from the dates and used in canning, and the dates can be distilled and used to make a strong beverage called *arak*.

FOOD AND DRINK

The Iraqis normally enjoy a rich and varied diet, although in recent years only the well-off can afford to eat well in the traditional manner. The diet includes a variety of vegetables and fruits, as well as meat, dairy products, and fish. The most popular traditional meat dishes are kebabs and *kubba*. Kebabs are pieces of lamb and tomatoes placed on a skewer and roasted over an open fire. *Kubba* are shells made with wheat and minced meat, and filled with more meat, nuts, onions, and spices, and then fried. Another Iraqi delicacy is called *masgouf*. It is fish caught in the Tigris River, and grilled on an open fire, often outdoors on the riverbank.

Other foods include cheese, eggs, and potatoes, which often make up the breakfast meal. A standard part of all meals is *samoons*, a round flat bread, and a drink made of unsweetened yogurt. Desserts include dates, melons, and fruits, and a pastry called *baklava*, which is made from thin sheets of pastry layered with nuts and honey. In addition to a yogurt drink, people enjoy a thick, sweet coffee, a sweetened lemon tea served in small glasses, and a strong beverage called *arak*, which is distilled from dates. People often eat meals together, traditionally while sitting on mats on the floor.

HOLIDAYS AND CELEBRATIONS

Food and drink play an important role in Iraqi holidays and celebrations. One of the most important religious celebrations is called the Id al Fitr, or the Feast of Fast Breaking. For one whole month—the month of Ramadan—devout Muslims fast. The Feast of Fast Breaking begins on the morning of the first day of the month following Ramadan and lasts for three days. During that time people gather with family and friends. They exchange gifts, pray together in congregations, and share large feasts. Some cities hold fairs during this time to celebrate the Feast of Fast Breaking.

National holidays include Army Day, January 6, which celebrates the founding of the army in 1921 and the importance of the military in society. Declaration of the Republic, July 14, celebrates the revolution of 1958 that overthrew the monarchy and established a republic with Abdul Karim Kassem at its head. Another national holiday is July 17, which celebrates the Peaceful Revolution of 1968 when the Baath Party came to power.

Another holiday that citizens are required to celebrate is April 28, the birthday of Saddam Hussein. The streets of Baghdad are decorated with neon lights, and people line the

Families gather to celebrate the Id al Fitr feast, marking the end of fasting during the Muslim holy month of Ramadan.

streets to watch the patriotic parades. A *Time* correspondent reports an interview with an Iraqi man and woman about Saddam's birthday celebration:

> When I asked him if anyone avoids the birthday parade, he looks at me as if I were daft. Anyone in Baghdad who has a job and wants to keep it shows up at the local parade and eats Saddam birthday cake. Smart people, says a woman, . . . know they have to go. Smart people, she says, want to live. [25]

THE MANY PROBLEMS FACING MODERN IRAQ

The entire way of life and the culture of the Iraqis have suffered in recent decades, not only from war but also from the dictatorial rule of Saddam Hussein, who is considered an outlaw by many Western nations. Iraq suffered devastating damage as a result of the Persian Gulf War and the later bombings. Once one of the most prosperous countries in the Middle East, the country faces enormous problems today. The economy is in shambles, with terrifically high rates of inflation and unemployment. The continued trade embargo against Iraq is causing enormous hardship for the Iraqi people.

Finally, the Western nations, particularly the United States, distrust Saddam Hussein. Although some experts disagree, some nations claim Saddam Hussein may be developing weapons of mass destruction and will possibly use them against Israel or sell them to terrorists for use in attacks against Western nations, such as the United States. Some nations, especially the United States, believe that Saddam Hussein should be ousted from office.

ECONOMIC SANCTIONS

The most pressing problem, which directly affects—or causes—Iraq's other serious problems, is the UN economic sanctions. When the allied forces won the Persian Gulf War, part of the cease-fire agreement was that Saddam Hussein would destroy his chemical and biological weapons and stop trying to produce nuclear weapons. UN inspectors were to be given freedom to inspect facilities in Iraq to be sure that the weapons had been destroyed. Once the destruction of weapons was verified by UN inspectors, the sanctions would be lifted and Iraq could once again export oil and use the money from oil to import goods. However, Saddam Hussein refused to allow inspectors in certain places and moved laboratories from place to place to avoid discovery. Because of

SADDAM THE NOVELIST

Though Saddam Hussein sleeps in a different location each night so he will not be assassinated and though most of his waking hours are devoted to ruling his country, the leader has found time to write two novels. The books, *Zabibah and the King* and *The Impregnable Fortress,* were published in Iraq without the author's name attached. Sources, including the CIA (which spent three months analyzing the first book), are fairly certain that Saddam is responsible, though many doubt he did all of the actual writing. Rather, it is speculated, professional writers were probably hired to write while Saddam oversaw the story.

Zabibah and the King is about a heroine, Zabibah, who represents the Iraqi people. Zabibah falls in love with the king, and they develop a chaste (nonphysical) relationship in which the benefits of a strict, autocratic government are discussed. One day, Zabibah is kidnapped and raped by her estranged ex-husband, and both are killed in a war with infidel invaders on January 17 (the day the Persian Gulf War started). The king avenges her death, proclaims her a martyr, and tries to piece together his country. However, different factions in the country make this impossible, and it is only after the king's death that the people realize his greatness.

The Impregnable Fortress, released just as *Zabibah and the King* was made into a play, received rave reviews from the Iraqi press (which is controlled by the government). Before its release, it was announced to be one of the best-selling books in the country's history. However, its sales have been poor, and as a result the government has made buying the book mandatory for many ordinary citizens of Iraq.

Though Iraqi sources have praised the books, most critics outside the country have had few positive words about them. And it appears that the people most interested in the books are not lovers of literature, but spies hoping for an insight into the mind of Saddam Hussein.

Saddam Hussein's lack of cooperation, the economic sanctions remain in place.

The majority of imported goods of all kinds are prevented from entering Iraq. Even though Iraq can import some food and medicines under the "oil-for-food" program, the sanctions still have serious effects. Goods and materials needed to repair the damage done to factories, roads, electric and sewage plants, and other damaged structures are severely restricted. Consumer goods such as electric appliances, automobile tires, and a host of other items are restricted. Without goods to sell or materials to operate businesses and factories, many businesses can no longer function. As long as these economic sanctions remain in place, Iraq has little chance of solving its other pressing problems.

The Damaged Infrastructure

Allied bombing during the Persian Gulf War and beginning again in 1998 had devastating effects on the country's infrastructure. Bridges and roads, electric power plants, water treatment plants (which also depend on electric power to operate), hospitals, and schools were destroyed or heavily damaged. According to a UN report shortly after the end of the war in 1991, Iraq had been bombed into the "pre-industrial age." The 1991 report reads in part:

An employee picks through the rubble of a bombed oil pumping facility after U.S.-led air strikes against Iraq in 1999.

Livestock farming has been seriously affected. . . . The sole laboratory producing veterinary vaccines was destroyed. All stocks of vaccine were destroyed in the bombardments on this center. . . . Prior to the crisis, Baghdad received about 450 liters of water [119 gal.] per person from seven treatment stations purifying water from the Tigris. With the destruction of power plants, oil refineries, main oil storage facilities and water-related chemical plants, all electrically operated installations have ceased to function. The supply of water in Baghdad has dropped to less than ten liters [2.5 gal] per day. Raw sewage is being dumped directly into the river—the source of the water supply.

Care for orphans, the elderly and the handicapped has been disrupted [at] . . . some 25 orphanages and 71 other social service centers. . . . Some 83 road bridges were de-

Iraqi citizens clear debris from homes hit by allied bombing in 2000. Air strikes have had devastating effects upon the country's infrastructure and citizens.

SADDAM AND THE ARAB WORLD

Saddam Hussein often attempts to portray himself as a champion of the Arab people. But the Arabs are a diverse group, and defining them as a single nation is a difficult task. Since the end of the Ottoman Empire, there has been a movement to unite all of the people who live under that name. It is this movement that Saddam Hussein hopes to use in his favor. If he can win the favor of Arabs from the Persian Gulf to North Africa, his power base would increase dramatically.

In some ways, he has been successful. There is growing discontent with Western influence in the Arab world. Although most Arabs did not see Saddam as a positive figure before the Gulf War, and his image was not improved when he invaded Kuwait, another Arab country, he has earned some grudging respect by defying the West, particularly the United States. A large part of this comes from Arab resentment of U.S. relations with Israel, an issue that carries great weight in the Middle East. It is primarily this issue that Saddam wishes to capitalize on (and a reason for firing Scud missiles on Israel, a neutral party, during the Gulf War).

While Arab governments may side with the United States—or at least do not oppose the United States—in its dealings with Iraq, many of the citizens of Arab countries are pro-Iraq. Demonstrations supporting Saddam have been held in Bahrain, Palestine, Lebanon, and other countries. Leaders of Arab states may not admire Saddam Hussein, but many people seem to side with Saddam Hussein in any conflict with the United States.

Arguably, Saddam is winning a public relations battle with the West when it comes to the people of Arab nations, though there is little chance that most Arabs wish Saddam to be their leader.

stroyed. Approximately 9,000 homes were destroyed or damaged beyond repair—2,500 in Baghdad and 1,900 in Basra. This has created a homeless potential of 72,000 persons. [26]

The Iran-Iraq and Persian Gulf wars also severely damaged Iraq's production of oil. The oil fields and the refineries were bombed, and pipelines were destroyed. Some oil pipelines and oil refineries have been restored, but the oil industry still needs large investments in equipment and repairs. Unless significant repairs are made, the production of oil will suffer, which means Iraq will generate even less revenue from export. Some electric service has been restored, but the electric production is just one-third of its 1990 capacity. Furthermore, an adequate level of water treatment and sewage plants has not been restored.

Most of the social infrastructure such as hospitals and schools is still in disrepair. Even though there is an "oil-for-

 ## WEAPONS OF MASS DESTRUCTION

Iraq has been accused of stockpiling weapons of mass destruction for over a decade. These weapons fall into three main classes: chemical, biological, and nuclear weapons.

The term "chemical weapons" is usually used to describe chemical agents, which are any liquid or gas that can be used in warfare to harm human beings. One of the first major examples of their use was during World War I, when German forces employed chlorine gas against the French. After the war, the third Geneva Convention made the use of chemical weapons against international law. Even though their use is illegal (and they have not been used in conventional warfare), chemical weapons technology has advanced considerably since that time.

Biological weapons are weapons capable of spreading infectious diseases that may harm or kill humans or animals. The use of biological warfare is very old. In ancient times, an army would hurl diseased corpses into a besieged city, in the hopes of spreading disease. (It is speculated that the Black Death was spread in this way.) No widespread use of biological weapons has taken place in the twentieth century, though many nations have developed programs to develop or refine deadly diseases, such as anthrax and smallpox. The use of biological weapons is also banned under the Geneva Convention.

Nuclear weapons are weapons that derive their destructive force from splitting or fusing atoms, a process that releases a tremendous amount of energy. Nuclear weapons have been used only once in the history of warfare: by the United States at the end of World War II. Since this time, the technology surrounding nuclear weapons has increased their power immensely. Only a few countries possess the technology to create nuclear weapons, but several smaller nations have been trying to acquire them in the last few decades.

food" program, the goods imported are strictly monitored. Any items that can possibly be used by the military or to rebuild plants that manufacture biological or chemical weapons are banned. This hinders the repair of water and sewage treatment plants, since chemicals are required. In addition, much of the medicines and other goods purchased for "humanitarian" purposes are diverted by the corrupt Hussein government for its own enrichment. Meanwhile, Saddam Hussein's government also sells Iraqi oil at cut-rate prices to neighboring countries such as Jordan and Syria. In return, those countries sell Iraqi goods that it cannot otherwise get. However, most of those goods, and the profits from the sale of oil, go directly to Saddam and his officials. Money that should be going to rebuild the country is going to build Saddam's palaces.

The International Committee of the Red Cross (ICRC) has attempted to help rebuild some of the infrastructure related to public health. According to Michel Minnig, former ICRC head of the delegation to Baghdad, the oil-for-food program covers some basic needs for food and medicine, "but this has no effect on the country's deteriorating infrastructure. In hospitals, for example, most of the bulbs in operating [room] lamps are broken and basic tools such as sterilizers are out of order." [27]

A DAMAGED ECONOMY

The problems caused by damaged infrastructure are compounded by the problem of the severely damaged economy. During the 1970s, Iraq was building a prosperous economy, fueled mainly by oil exports. Before the war with Iran, Iraq was second only to Saudi Arabia in the production of oil. Now the combination of the UN sanctions, the destruction of infrastructure, and Saddam's diversion of oil income to his own use has severely damaged Iraq's economy, causing inflation, unemployment, destruction of the middle class, and crime.

For more than a decade, Iraq has suffered severe inflation. For example, prices of goods and services rose 1,500–2,000 times between August 1990 and August 1991, following the Persian Gulf War. Prices have continued to rise at astronomical rates since then. At first the government tried to help government employees keep up with rising prices by giving them enormous raises in salaries, but inflation quickly ate up the increases. Now the high salaries are reserved for special army personnel and civil servants. Government workers who are members of the Baath Party for ten years or more receive much higher salaries than other government workers with similar jobs. Military officers receive much higher salaries than government workers, and members of Saddam Hussein's own Republican Guards receive the highest salaries of all.

The Iraqi currency—the dinar—is almost worthless. Inflation increased at such a rate that by 1995, a pound of meat cost a family the equivalent of $500 U.S. dollars. A carton of eggs cost more than $1000. By 2002, according to a *Time* magazine reporter who visited Iraq, "A woman I will call Layla . . . quit her [equivalent to] $2-a-month office job because it wasn't worth getting up in the morning." [28] Monthly food rations from the oil-for-food program are not sufficient for most families. Food shops may have supplies, but 90 percent of the people are unable to afford them. An egg, for example, can cost a week's wages. Those who are fortunate have relatives in other countries who can send money. Layla depends upon her brother in Florida to send her extra money, but others must beg, steal, or work several jobs just to eat.

Karim, who runs a car-alarm business, is unable to feed his family of four on his monthly food rations. But the elite in Iraqi society can afford to spend $45 on a car alarm system to protect their new cars. The money he earns helps him occasionally buy a little meat for his family. Few people can survive on their salary alone. Adnan Zaki works at a Baghdad hospital. His monthly salary of 3,000 dinars is worth about $2.50 in U.S. dollars. He works any odd jobs he can find to feed his family. A Canadian visitor to Baghdad reports: "I change $50 [U.S. dollars] and receive a bagful of nearly worthless Iraqi dinars in return. Paying our [check at a restaurant] takes us 10 minutes just to count through the 400-odd banknotes [bills]." [29]

The damage to the economy has caused a marked rise in crime. In 1995 an Iraqi professional living in New York City returned to Iraq for a visit and reported the following:

The embargo has destroyed the fabric of society, bringing robbery, rape and highway brigandage in its tow. Two old ladies in our neighborhood have had their houses burgled three times in a month. A cousin who was abroad had her house stripped down to the electri-

cal outlets. Another relation, stopping at a traffic light, was amazed by a young man who got into her car, said hello and then started to push her out—all in broad daylight and on a main street. Now everyone locks the car doors from the inside before driving out the front gates.[30]

Children sift through a garbage heap in search of food. UN sanctions and Iraq's governmental corruption have created a scarcity of many necessities.

UNEMPLOYMENT AND ITS CONSEQUENCES

Even at the low wages and high inflation, there is high unemployment. In some regions the unemployment rate is 70 percent. Millions of people are now unemployed or employed part-time. Others hold two or three jobs just to keep themselves and their families fed. As the family income declines, children are often put to work doing odd jobs such as delivering packages, carrying groceries, or selling items on street

A boy sells bananas at a well-frequented square. Under present economic conditions in Iraq, trade and manual labor earn higher wages than teaching and medicine.

corners. In many cases, children drop out of school to help their families survive.

The high unemployment coupled with the incredible inflation has led to the impoverishment of the middle class. Even formerly affluent middle-class families feel the pinch, and the selling off of family silver or household items at flea markets is a common occurrence. The new rich are the illegal traders and smugglers and the elite government employees. The once well-off professional classes have trouble earning a living. According to one writer,

> It is apparently easier to make a living today from trade or manual employment—or by theft, illegal trading and bribery—than it is being a professor, doctor, teacher or even engineer. In 1993, a thirty-year-old civil engineer working as a taxi driver was quoted as saying: "Now education is no use. As an engineer I would earn 30 dinars

a month; now as a taxi driver I can earn 4000 dinars. And I absolutely need 4000." The article further commented, "Mechanics and vegetable and grain sellers are making new fortunes. In contrast, engineers, writers, pharmacists, travel operators, technical consultants, scientists and surgeons find themselves without work."[31]

EDUCATION

What was once Iraq's pride, the education system, is near collapse. Children attend classes in buildings that are decaying and where equipment and materials are not replaced. Sanctions have meant that schools are having trouble getting supplies as simple as pencils and paper. Many children drop out of school early and do not go on to higher education. Children who were once sent to school are now sent to work on farms or in factories to help feed the family. Enrollment in primary school—once nearly 100 percent—is down to 88 percent for boys and 79 percent for girls. Adult literacy rates have dropped as well.

Students able to go on to higher education suffer as well. For example, Western researchers working with young Iraq archaeologists excavating ancient sites fear that this new generation does not have up-to-date knowledge about the latest methods and technology. Medical schools lack proper teaching equipment. Textbooks in nearly all areas of higher education are out of date by years.

This decline in education will be felt by Iraqi society for at least a generation. The damage to the environment may last even longer.

ENVIRONMENTAL PROBLEMS

Water and air pollution are two serious environmental problems in Iraq. Destruction of sewage treatment plants has led to serious water pollution in the Tigris and Euphrates rivers, which the city of Baghdad depends upon as sources of water. Water treatment plants cannot import chlorine, the chemical most necessary to purify water. Air pollution in the cities is caused by poorly maintained motor vehicles.

However, one of the most serious environmental problems stems from Iraqi government policies. Over the past two decades, a crisis has been building in the marshlands. The building of dams and irrigation systems to provide water for

Iraq's growing population has cut down on the flow of water to the marshes. In addition, Iraq has undertaken a plan to drain the marshes and use the land for agriculture. Pictures from space show that the marshlands have diminished by 90 percent over the past 25 years. Many of the Madan, or Marsh Arabs, who have depended upon this environment for thousands of years, have been forced to move.

Not only the people but the animals have suffered from the drying up of the marshlands. Migrating birds, waterfowl, and animals such as the otter are all at risk. According to Klaus Toepfer, director of the United Nations Environment Program, "This major ecological disaster [is] comparable to the drying up of the Aral Sea [a large saltwater lake in Kazakhstan and Uzbekistan] and the deforestation of large tracts of Amazonia [in the Brazilian rain forest]." [32]

In addition to the damage to the environment and the severe suffering the Iraqi people have endured from the effects of war and economic sanctions, the people also suffer at the hands of their own government.

HUMAN RIGHTS ABUSES

Since the rise of Saddam Hussein, international and internal Iraqi sources have documented a variety of serious human rights violations in Iraq. Though the true scope of these violations is unknown, there is more than enough proof that atrocities have occurred under Saddam's regime. Groups like the Kurds, whom Saddam considers blood enemies, as well as all other citizens of Iraq are subject to government brutality.

Some abuses have occurred during war or have been committed by Saddam's armed forces. Over the last two decades, conflicts with the Kurds and Iranians have produced large minefields in northern Iraq. These minefields, which are located in areas that contain many innocent civilians, continue to maim and kill ordinary people long after the wars in which they were planted have ended. After the Persian Gulf War, when Saddam faced serious opposition from Shiites and Kurds, government forces not only brutally crushed the resistance by using far superior military technology but often killed women and children indiscriminately to punish the rebel groups.

The government has also implemented brutal punishments for relatively minor criminal offenses. Such crimes as

Iraqi president Saddam Hussein appears at a military function in 2001. Under Saddam's tyrannical rule Iraq's citizens have experienced poverty and many abuses.

bribery and theft can warrant vicious treatment, including amputation, branding, and even death.

Speaking out against the government can bring the most serious punishment. For even slight amounts of dissent, Saddam's regime has relocated, by force, entire families of those who would speak against him (or those whom he thinks have spoken against him). People have disappeared after being reported as antigovernment by their neighbors. In many of these cases, there has been little or no proof of any crime. Political prisoners are routinely tortured, and thousands of people, including children, have been executed. Saddam's offenses against his own people, as well as his threat to the rest of the world, have made him an outlaw among world leaders.

SADDAM AND THE WESTERN POWERS

Some might argue that Iraq's biggest problem is its leader, Saddam Hussein. Today, Saddam Hussein is the absolute dictator of Iraq, a tyrant who rules with the iron hand of terror. He surrounds himself with relatives and friends from his town of Tikrit. He rewards them with big salaries and fine cars and homes. No one—from the highest government official to the lowliest peasant—dares to oppose him or criticize him in any way. He is ruthless in wiping out opposition, even killing his own family members who oppose him. Furthermore, he has shown in the past that he is willing and able to produce weapons of mass destruction and to use them.

The Western powers would like to see Saddam Hussein removed from office. The United States in particular has made it clear that its goal is to remove Saddam and replace his regime with a more democratic government, one that would dismantle any weapons of mass destruction and not be a threat to its neighbors.

Undoubtedly, Saddam Hussein is a tyrannical dictator. At the same time, he has been the only leader in decades who has been able to maintain his power and keep the country united. If Saddam Hussein is removed, it is not clear who would replace him. Since its establishment as a republic, Iraq has not had a democratic and stable government. With Saddam gone, Iraq may see a series of military coups d'etat, as has happened before. The question remains whether the Western powers will be able to install a regime that can unify the Iraqi people, and whether they can guarantee that Saddam's successor will not be as brutal as he is.

In November 2002, UN weapons inspectors returned to Iraq, in accordance with a resolution passed by the United Nations Security Council, under pressure from the United States. The inspectors' job is to look for evidence of weapons of mass destruction and to determine that Iraq has destroyed all such weapons. The United States has made clear that should Iraq not cooperate fully with the inspectors, the United States and its allies will attack Iraq and remove Saddam Hussein and his regime from power. While some nations agree with the position of the United States, many nations are opposed to war. How many nations of the world will support a U.S. war against Iraq is uncertain.

One thing is certain—until the Western nations are sure that the Iraqi government has dismantled and destroyed all of its dangerous weapons and until the trade embargo is lifted so that Iraqis can freely sell their oil and import necessary goods, the problems and suffering of the Iraqi people will continue. Many experts believe it is unlikely that Saddam Hussein will satisfactorily cooperate with the UN inspectors and that war is inevitable. Whether the forcible removal of Saddam Hussein from power will ultimately solve the problems of Iraq and its people or whether it will create even further problems for Iraq and other countries of the Middle East remains to be seen.

FACTS ABOUT IRAQ

GEOGRAPHY

Location: Middle East, bordering Persian Gulf, between Kuwait and Iran; bordered by Turkey, Iran, Kuwait, Saudi Arabia, Jordan, and Syria

Total area (includes land and water): 167,975 square miles (437,072 square km)

Comparative area: Slightly more than twice the size of the state of Idaho

Coastline: 36 miles (58 km)

Climate: mainly desert; mild to cool winters; dry, hot summers; northern mountainous regions have cold winters with occasionally heavy snows; snow melt in spring can cause serious flooding in central and southern Iraq

Terrain: reedy marshes in southeast; broad plains in central area; mountains in northern borders with Turkey and Iran

Natural resources: petroleum, natural gas, phosphates, sulfur

Land use: 12%, arable land; 9%, permanent pastures; 0%, permanent crops; 0%, forests; 79%, other

PEOPLE

Population: 23,331,985 (July 2001 estimate)

Ethnic groups: 75%–80%, Arab; 15%–29%, Kurdish; 5%, Turkoman, Assyrian, and other

Religions: 97%, Muslim (Shia 60%–65%, Sunni 32%–37%); 3%, Christian and other

Languages: Arabic, Kurdish, Assyrian, Armenian

GOVERNMENT

Type: republic

Capital: Baghdad

Chief of State: President (Saddam Hussein since July 1979)

Head of Government: Prime Minister (Saddam Hussein since May 1994)

Political parties: Baath Party, controlled by Revolutionary Command Council (RCC) (Saddam Hussein, Chairman)

Legal system: Islamic law in special religious courts; civil law system elsewhere

Flag description: three equal horizontal bands of red, white, and black; three green five-pointed starts in a horizontal line centered in the white band, with the phrase "Allahu Akbar" ("God is Great") in the white band

ECONOMY

Overview: Petroleum industry dominates, traditionally accounts for 95% of foreign exchange earnings. 1980–1988 war with Iran caused massive expenditures and damage to oil facilities; economic sanctions following Iraq's invasion of Kuwait, subsequent damage from Persian Gulf War dramatically reduced economic activity. Per capita output and living standards still far below pre-war levels.

Agricultural products: wheat, barley, rice, vegetables, dates, cotton; sheep, cattle

Exports: crude oil

Imports: food, medicine, manufactured goods

NOTES

INTRODUCTION

1. Quoted in Geoff Simons, *Iraq: From Sumer to Saddam.* New York: St. Martin's Press, 1994, p. 79.

CHAPTER 2: THE PEOPLE OF IRAQ

2. Steve Tamari, "Who are the Arabs?" www.ccasonline.org.

3. Dr. Vera Saeedpour, "Meet the Kurds." www.cobblestone pub.com.

4. Quoted in BBCi, "The Marsh Arabs." www.bbc.co.uk.

CHAPTER 3: THE CRADLE OF CIVILIZATION

5. Quoted in Simons, *Iraq: From Sumer to Saddam,* p. 85.

6. Quoted in Simons, *Iraq: From Sumer to Saddam,* p. 88.

7. Quoted in Simons, *Iraq: From Sumer to Saddam,* p. 90.

8. Quoted in Simons, *Iraq: From Sumer to Saddam,* p. 91.

9. Quoted in Seton Lloyd, *Ruined Cities of Iraq.* Chicago: Ares Publishers, 1980, p. 60.

10. Quoted in Simons, *Iraq: From Sumer to Saddam,* p. 135.

11. Quoted in Simons, *Iraq: From Sumer to Saddam,* p. 135.

CHAPTER 4: WESTERN INFLUENCE AND THE MODERN WORLD

12. Quoted in William Spencer, *Iraq: Old Land, New Nation in Conflict.* Brookfield, CT: Twenty-First Century Books, 2000, pp. 64–65.

13. Quoted in Simons, *Iraq: From Sumer to Saddam,* pp. 219–20.

14. Simons, *Iraq: From Sumer to Saddam,* p. 248.

CHAPTER 5: THE IRAQI WAY OF LIFE

15. "Surviving Sanctions," *Economist,* December 12, 1998, p. 47.

16. Colin Rowat, "How the Sanctions Hurt Iraq," MERIP Press Information Note 65, August 2, 2001.

17. Quoted in Heidi Schlumpf, "Collateral Damage," *U.S. Catholic,* August 2001, p. 38.

18. "The Iraq Diaries," *Maclean's,* February 26, 2001, p. 24.

19. "The Iraq Diaries," p. 24.

20. "The Iraq Diaries," p. 24.

21. Peter Kandela, "Effects of Sanctions on Iraq's Health Professionals," *Lancet,* April 19, 1997, p. 1153.

CHAPTER 6: CULTURE IN IRAQ

22. Quoted in "The Fast of Ramadan." www.holidays.net.

23. Quoted in Andrew Dampf, "Iraq's Soccer Team Tours Italy," www.iraqsport.com. August 14, 2002.

24. Quoted in Dampf, "Iraq's Soccer Team Tours Italy."

25. Johanna McGeary, "Inside Saddam's New Charm Offensive," www.Time.Com. May 3, 2002.

CHAPTER 7: THE MANY PROBLEMS FACING MODERN IRAQ

26. Quoted in Ian Peters, "UN Reports Iraq Bombed into 'Pre-Industrial Age,'" *Earth Island Journal,* Spring 1991, p. 48.

27. Quoted in "Iraq: Decaying Infrastructure Raises Concern for the Population," *ICRC News,* July 29, 1999.

28. McGeary, "Inside Saddam's New Charm Offensive."

29. "The Iraq Diaries," p. 24.

30. Selma Al-Radi, "Iraqi Sanctions—A Postwar Crime," *Nation,* March 27, 1995, p. 416.

31. Sarah Graham-Brown, *Sanctioning Saddam: The Politics of Intervention in Iraq.* New York: I.B. Tauris, 1999, p. 183.

32. Quoted in Tom Radford, "The Age: Iraqi Marsh Arabs See Lifeblood Drain Away," www.theage.com. May 20, 2001.

CHRONOLOGY

3500 B.C.
Sumerians establish first true cities in Mesopotamia; Sumerians develop writing, use the wheel.

2330
Akkadians conquer Sumer. Sargon the Great establishes the first known empire.

2100–2000
Ur establishes dominance in southern Mesopotamia.

2006
The civilization of Ur is destroyed.

1792
Hammurabi comes to power as ruler of Babylonia.

1595
Hammurabi dynasty falls to nomadic tribes.

800s
Assyrians begin building an empire.

612
Ninveh, capital of Assyria, falls.

600
Nebuchadnezzar rebuilds Babylon and establishes a new Babylonian kingdom.

539
Persian King Cyrus the Great conquers Babylonia.

331
Alexander the Great conquers Babylon, bringing Greek culture.

570 A.D.
The prophet Muhammad is born.

637
Arabs conquer region and establish an Islamic Empire.

762
Abbasid Caliphate establishes Baghdad as capital of Islamic empire.

1258
Mongols invade and destroy Baghdad.

1534
Ottoman Turks capture Baghdad and conquer Mesopotamia.

1914
World War I begins; Ottomans join the war on German side.

1918
World War I ends; Ottoman Empire collapses.

1920
Great Britain assumes rule of Iraq under League of Nations Mandate.

1921
King Faisal takes the throne in Iraq.

1927
Oil discovered in Iraq.

1932
Iraq becomes independent nation and member of League of Nations.

1958
Iraqi army overthrows monarchy.

1968
Iraqi Baath Party takes control of government.

1979
Saddam Hussein assumes control of government.

1980–1988
War between Iraq and Iran.

1990
Iraq invades Kuwait.

1991
Persian Gulf War.

1998

United Nations weapons inspectors leave Iraq; U.S. and British forces resume bombing military installations.

2002

Saddam Hussein accused of building weapons of mass destruction; U.N. sends weapons inspectors in December.

FOR FURTHER READING

Said K. Aburish, *Saddam Hussein: The Politics of Revenge.* London: Bloomsbury, 2000. Unusual perspective on the psychology behind the Iraqi dictator. The author has extensive knowledge of the Arab world and writes from both the Arab and Western (mainly British) perspectives.

J.P. Docherty, *Iraq.* Philadelphia: Chelsea House, 1999. An overview of Iraq for young people.

Leila Merrell Foster, *Iraq: Enchantment of the World.* New York: Childrens Press, 1998. Full of color photographs, this book gives an overview of Iraq for young people, including a description of a typical day for an Iraqi youngster.

Sarah Graham-Brown, *Sanctioning Saddam: The Politics of Intervention in Iraq.* New York: I.B. Tauris, 1999. Heavily footnoted, this book gives detailed insight into the consequences for Iraq of economic sanctions and international humanitarian aid.

Dawn Kotapish, *Daily Life in Ancient and Modern Baghdad.* Minneapolis: Runestone Press, a division of Lerner Publishing Group, 2000. Young readers will enjoy this brightly illustrated book filled with details of life in this ancient capital city of Iraq.

Samuel Noah Kramer and editors of Time-Life Books, *Cradle of Civilization.* New York: Time-Life Books, 1967. A beautifully illustrated overview of ancient Mesopotamia.

Lerner Publishing Group, Geography Department, *Iraq in Pictures.* Minneapolis: Lerner Publications, rev. ed., 1992. An appealing book with concise information on the geography, history, people, and economy of Iraq. Filled with color and black-and-white visuals.

Gail B. Stewart, *Iraq.* New York: Crestwood House, 1991. Suitable for young readers, this book focuses on Iraq during the Persian Gulf War, with a brief overview of Iraq's history.

Editors of Time-Life Books, *Mesopotamia: The Mighty Kings.* Alexandria, VA: Time-Life Books, 1995. An overview of ancient Mesopotamia through the conquest by Alexander the Great, including many pictures of ancient artifacts.

WORKS CONSULTED

BOOKS

Frederick W. Axelgard, ed., *Iraq in Transition: A Political, Economic, and Strategic Perspective.* Boulder, CO: Westview Press, in cooperation with the Center for Strategic and International Studies, Georgetown University, 1986. This scholarly series of articles analyzing changes that occurred in U.S.-Iraq relations under Saddam Hussein's leadership gives insight into Iraq's role in the Middle East.

Martin A. Beek, translated by D.R. Welsh, *Atlas of Mesopotamia.* New York: Thomas Nelson and Sons, 1962. An overview of Mesopotamian civilization from the Stone Age through the conquest by Alexander the Great. Many maps, pictures, and excerpts from ancient texts.

Marion Farouk-Sluglett and Peter Sluglett, *Iraq Since 1958: From Revolution to Dictatorship.* New York: I.B. Tauris, 1990. A historical analysis of the rise of modern Iraq up to Iraq's invasion of Kuwait.

Waldemar J. Gallman, *Iraq Under General Nuri: My Recollections of Nuri Al-Said, 1954–1958.* Baltimore: Johns Hopkins University Press, 1964. Recollections of former U.S. ambassador to Iraq about Nuri al-Said, an Iraqi statesman and leader during the 1950s.

Sarah Graham-Brown, *Sanctioning Saddam: The Politics of Intervention in Iraq.* New York: I.B. Tauris, 1999. Discussion of the consequences for Iraq of economic sanctions and international humanitarian aid.

Avigdor Haselkorn, *The Continuing Storm: Iraq, Poisonous Weapons, and Deterrence.* New Haven: Yale University Press, 1999. Focuses on how chemical and biological weapons affected the Gulf War and how Iraq's possession of weapons of mass destruction affects world politics.

Efraim Karsh and Inari Rautsi, *Saddam Hussein: A Political Biography.* New York: Free Press, 1991. Detailed in-depth insights into the mind of the Iraqi dictator.

Seton Lloyd, *Ruined Cities of Iraq.* Chicago: Ares Publishers, 1980. A discussion of ancient cities of Iraq, focusing on archaeological excavations.

Helen Chapin Metz, ed., *Iraq a Country Study.* Washington, DC: Federal Research Division of Library of Congress, 1990. Government publication giving detailed overview focused primarily on modern Iraq. Includes many tables of statistics.

A. Leo Oppenheim, trans., *Letters From Mesopotamia.* Chicago: University of Chicago Press, 1967. A collection of private and official letters from ancient Mesopotamia that reveals intimate details about life in the ancient Near East.

Geoff Simons, *Iraq: From Sumer to Saddam.* New York: St. Martin's Press, 1994. A general history of Iraq from ancient times to the 1990s, with special attention to modern-day Iraq.

William Spencer, *Iraq: Old Land, New Nation in Conflict.* Brookfield, CT: Twenty-First Century Books, 2000. Traces Iraq's history from ancient Mesopotamia to its modern political problems.

PERIODICALS

Selma Al-Radi, "Iraqi Sanctions—A Postwar Crime," *Nation,* March 27, 1995.

Mark Bowden, "Tales of the Tyrant," *Atlantic Monthly,* May 2002.

"Iraq: Decaying Infrastructure Raises Concern for the Population," *ICRC News,* July 29, 1999.

"The Iraq Diaries," *Maclean's,* February 26, 2001.

Peter Kandela, "Effects of Sanctions on Iraq's Health Professionals," *Lancet,* April 19, 1997.

Ian Peters, "UN Reports Iraq Bombed into 'Pre-Industrial Age,'" *Earth Island Journal,* Spring 1991.

Colin Rowat, "How the Sanctions Hurt Iraq," MERIP Press Information Note 65, August 2, 2001.

Michael Rubin, "Food Fight," *New Republic,* June 18, 2001.

Heidi Schlumpf, "Collateral Damage," *U.S. Catholic,* August 2001.

"Surviving Sanctions," *Economist,* December 12, 1998.

INTERNET SOURCES

Andrew Dampf, "Iraq's Soccer Team Tours Italy," August 14, 2002. www.iraqsport.com.

"Dictionary of Islamic Architecture." www.archnet.org.

"The Fast of Ramadan." www.holidays.net.

"The Marsh Arabs," BBCi. www.bbc.co.uk.

Johanna McGeary, "Inside Saddam's New Charm Offensive," May 3, 2002. www.Time.Com.

Tom Radford, "The Age: Iraqi Marsh Arabs See Lifeblood Drain Away," May 20, 2001. www.theage.com.

Dr. Vera Saeedpour, "Meet the Kurds." www.cobblestonepub. com.

Steve Tamari, "Who are the Arabs?" www.ccasonline.org.

WEBSITES

Arab Net (www.arab.net). A source of information about Arab countries, including up-to-date news articles.

Geographia (www.geographia.com). Articles about the people and culture of a variety of regions of the world.

Iraq Net (www.iraq.net). Iraq's official website, which includes a variety of information about the country and its people.

The World Factbook (www.cia.gov). A source of statistical information and facts about nations of the world.

INDEX

Picture Credits

About the Author

Phyllis Corzine earned a bachelor's degree in literature and language from Webster University and a master's degree in English and American literature from Washington University in St. Louis. She worked as an editor of educational materials for elementary and high school students for five years.

For the past twelve years, she has taught English and worked as a freelance writer. She has written four previous books for Lucent. Her other work includes a variety of educational materials, as well as *Eddie's Magic Radio,* a fantasy novel for young adults. Corzine lives with her husband in St. Louis. She has three children and six grandchildren. In her spare time she enjoys reading, gardening, and tennis.